The Quiet Rebel

A Memoir of My Peace Corps Adventures in Bolivia

Peggy Dickenson

The Quiet Rebel Press
Sarasota, Florida

The Quiet Rebel:
A Memoir of My
Peace Corps
Adventures in Bolivia

Written by Peggy Dickenson

Copyright © 2013

ISBN 978-0-615-72893-3

First Edition: 2013

Printed in the United States of America

Inquiries and Orders may be sent to:
The Quiet Rebel Press
1235 Tallywood Drive
Sarasota, Florida 34237-3226
U.S.A.

For additional information and online ordering,
contact: dellis6245@aol.com

Dedicated to my mother
who encouraged my unconventional
life of travel and adventure. By
following my heart, I escaped the call
to settle down, marry, and procreate,
and thus, she named me "The Quiet Rebel."

Llamas

"Life in the Peace Corps will not be easy. There will be no salary, and allowances will be at a level sufficient only to maintain health and meet basic needs. Men and women will be expected to work and live alongside the nationals of the country in which they are stationed – doing the same work, eating the same food, talking the same language.

"But if the life will not be easy, it will be rich and satisfying. For every young American who participates in the Peace Corps – who works in a foreign land – will know that he or she is sharing in the great common task of bringing to man that decent way of life which is the foundation of freedom and a condition of peace."

John F. Kennedy
35th President of the United States
and Founder of the Peace Corps

Pre-Incan stone face

ACKNOWLEDGMENTS

As I look back at the age of 70, the two years I served as a Peace Corps Volunteer in Bolivia were the most exciting and challenging of my life. My purpose in writing this book was to share that experience with family and friends and to inspire young men and especially young women to do the same.

By giving a year or two or just a few months to a non-profit organization such as the Peace Corps, Teach For America, Habitat for Humanity, Smile Train, or KIVA (a micro-finance organization), your life will be richer for it, and you'll receive more in return than you could ever imagine. I certainly did.

During the five years I worked on this book, many friends helped me through it. First, I wish to thank my husband, Don Ellis, for his support, encouragement, and editing advice as he patiently read each chapter. Second, I thank Archie Bruun, my Bolivian co-worker in the Peace Corps office in Santa Cruz, Bolivia, for his excellent memory about events that happened to me when I lived there. Thanks also to his wife, Marty Bruun, and fellow Peace Corps Volunteers John Guy and Margaret Mimna Cummings for sharing their memories.

Others who encouraged me in this process include Lee and Russ Heitz, with special thanks to Russ for his editing and publishing expertise, Rosemary Novak, Dollie Mancilla, Carole and Dave Munro, Keith Reckling, and my sister, Elizabeth Rudolf. I'm indebted to you all.

Panpipes
musical instrument

TABLE OF CONTENTS

Chapter 1 – Peace Corps Training.............. Page 1
Chapter 2 – The Adventure Begins............. Page 9
Chapter 3 – The La Paz Office .... Page 12
Chapter 4 – Settling In .... Page 15
Chapter 5 – La Paz Calling Santa Cruz .... Page 19
Chapter 6 – Dancing at 12,000 Feet
                        Above Sea Level....................... Page 24
Chapter 7 – The Bullfight .... Page 28
Chapter 8 – Culture Shock .... Page 31
Chapter 9 – The Black Market .... Page 36
Chapter 10 – Tupac Katari University .... Page 41
Chapter 11 – A Trip on the *Altiplano*........... Page 47
Chapter 12 – The ABCs of Literacy .... Page 54
Chapter 13 – *Carnaval* in Oruro .... Page 59
Chapter 14 – Teaching in El Alto .... Page 65
Chapter 15 – The Other Copacabana.......... Page 70
Chapter 16 – Getting In Over My Head........ Page 75
Chapter 17 – A Revealing Day on
                        Ipanema Beach .... Page 79
Chapter 18 – A Derby for Rip Kirby............. Page 86
Chapter 19 – A Special Visit to El Alto .... Page 93
Chapter 20 – Magical Machu Picchu .... Page 98
Chapter 21 – Transfer to Santa Cruz .... Page 104
Chapter 22 – Hot Temperatures and
                        Cold Showers....................... Page 110
Chapter 23 – The Virgin of Cotoca.............. Page 115
Chapter 24 – *El Caballito* Nightclub .... Page 120
Chapter 25 – *Carnaval* in Santa Cruz .... Page 124
Chapter 26 – Lucho .... Page 129
Chapter 27 – Meeting the Chief Justice .... Page 133
Chapter 28 – Searching for Che Guevara.... Page 135
Chapter 29 – More Culture Shock................ Page 141
Chapter 30 – *Vaya Con Dios* (Go With
                        God) .... Page 145

Willys Jeep

BOLIVIA
1965-1967

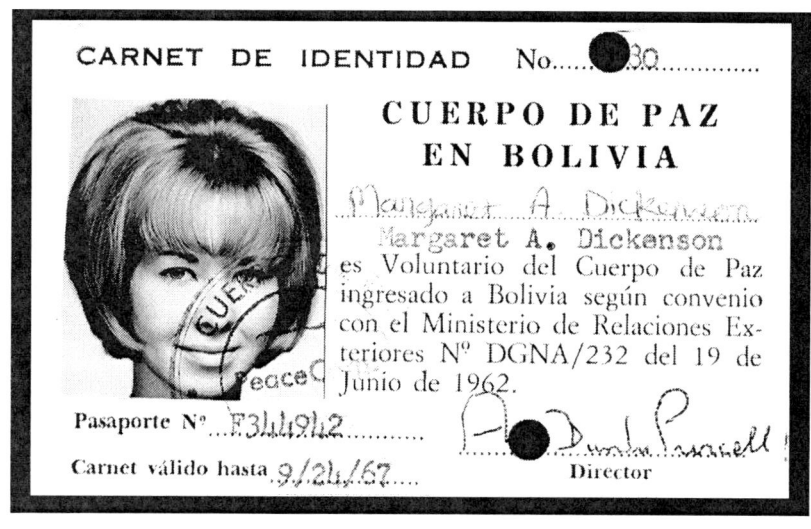

My Bolivian ID card which identifies
me as a Peace Corps Volunteer.

Toucan bird

Cartoon from *The New Yorker*

*"Why aren't you out doing good in the
wilds of Bolivia or somewhere?"*

Palm trees

CHAPTER ONE
PEACE CORPS TRAINING

My two-year Bolivian adventure began in Tucson on June 19, 1965 when I reported for Peace Corps training at the University of Arizona, a beautiful campus of green palm trees and red brick buildings. The Peace Corps coordinator, a young woman in her 30s with her hair pulled back in a ponytail, warmly shook my hand as I entered her office, but her first words startled me. "*Hola, como se llama*?" (Hello, what is your name?), she asked. "*Me llamo* Peggy Dickenson," I heard myself answer, amazed to still remember my high school Spanish. But there was no time to congratulate myself, as the interview continued in Spanish, and I struggled to keep up.

Sink or swim – this was how training began for our group of 27 women in the Latin American Regional Program for Volunteer Secretaries. In a surprising move, the coordinator disappointed the five most fluent Spanish speakers by assigning them to Brazil, and they had to learn Portuguese instead. This odd decision was the start of a grueling, mentally-exhausting, two-month training period with classes in Spanish or Portuguese, health guidelines for third-world living, teaching English as a foreign language, and Latin American history, geography, and customs.

To prepare us for unsanitary conditions at our future posts, a doctor inoculated us each week against such exotic diseases as yellow fever, typhoid, diphtheria, and plague, plus two rabies shots in the abdomen. A typical day started at 5:45am and ended around midnight. The relentless cycle of classes, homework, and psychological scrutiny took its toll. This was brutal, the toughest experience I've ever had.

Survival swimming and physical exercise toughened us up, while stressful situations and psychological tests measured our mental well-being. One exercise required us to list five trainees we disliked and explain why. We all struggled to choose five of our comrades but later learned the joke was on us. Our choices were used to analyze us, not those on our lists, and we realized how closely we were being watched. It was unsettling.

Nevertheless, the camaraderie among us was strong as we supported each other through the process. These were wonderful women, all professional secretaries, mostly in their 20s, three in their 30s, and one 48-year-old. We had joined the Peace Corps for a variety of reasons, some idealistic, others looking for escape, adventure or travel, and all inspired by President John F. Kennedy, the founder of the Peace Corps, who had been assassinated two years earlier in 1963.

Before arriving in Tucson for Peace Corps training, I had earned a living for three years as a secretary in New York City. One evening, after working all day in the Deans Office of the Columbia University School of Engineering, I was heading for the subway when I made a fateful detour. As I stepped into a darkened auditorium where a film about the Peace Corps was being shown, I was mesmerized by what I saw on the screen. Here was a chance for adventure, romance,

2

and a way to make a meaningful contribution in the world. I immediately sent in my application and was quickly accepted as a trainee. Now here I was in Arizona, making my dream come true.

One of the trainees was a tall, young California woman named Sandy. She was my roommate and best friend. Witty and clever with a dose of irreverence, she made me laugh which helped relieve the stress. However, Sandy's laid-back attitude sometimes got her in trouble. She begged me to shine the light in her eyes every morning and nag her until she got up, but Sandy was never awake by the time I left for breakfast. Nevertheless, she always managed to breeze into class just in the nick of time.

I sing in a dorm room at the University of Arizona for my friends during Peace Corps training. July 1965

Mornings were especially difficult for us, because there were too many temptations at night. Our dormitory housed a group of young Latin American men studying English for the summer. The men's rooms were on one side of the dormitory and the women's on the other. A recreation room in between,

3

furnished with couches, chairs, and tables, brought us together, and it didn't take long for us to find each other and practice our new language skills. As a way to break the ice, I brought my guitar to the recreation room and we sang American folk songs -- *Blowing in the Wind*; *Puff, the Magic Dragon*; and *This Land is Your Land*.

Among the Latin American men was a tall, gregarious, chubby young man from El Salvador named Roberto whose cute Spanish accent and disarming personality made him popular with everyone. After classes and homework, Roberto and I often spent the evening together either in the recreation room listening to his records of Eydie Gorme singing in Spanish with the trio Los Panchos or at a local bar called The Green Dolphin.

One evening, as Roberto and I sat in a booth at the bar, drinking beer and listening to the jukebox, a Peace Corps trainee named Becky and one of the young Latin American men joined us. We all spoke in English, but suddenly, the two men switched to Spanish, assuming we couldn't understand them. They discussed kissing our lovely, long necks, but to my surprise I understood every word and teased them about it. The guys sheepishly laughed and looked at me with a new-found respect for my limited but burgeoning Spanish skills

And so the summer progressed until training ended on August 28, 1965 when we silently filed into a conference room to learn if we had graduated. As we sat around a large table, we stared wide-eyed at each other. Everyone was scared. All the sound had been sucked out of the room, and I could hardly breathe.

Finally, the Peace Corps coordinator ended the suspense and congratulated all of us on becoming Peace Corps Volunteers. There was a collective sigh of relief until we realized three members of our group were missing.

One of them named Karen had given me a valuable gift the night before -- a small black transistor radio, the height of technology at the time. Now I understood why she had insisted I take it -- she knew she was leaving the program but couldn't tell me. Sadly I never saw her again and never had the chance to say goodbye. As for the other two women, one had transferred to a Peace Corps training program for community development rather than serve as a Volunteer secretary, and the other had dropped out or been dismissed.

As Peace Corps Volunteers, we now received our host country assignments. Mine was Bolivia, and Sandy's was Chile. A young woman named Maryann was also assigned to Bolivia. She was friendly and kind but seemed a little awkward to some of the more critical members of our group. At the graduation party, the Peace Corps coordinator took me aside and confided, "We assigned Maryann with you, because we know you'll be nice to her."

During two weeks vacation back home in Chappaqua, a suburb of New York City, I said goodbye to my family and friends and fielded concerns about the Peace Corps and living in South America. My mother, a trailblazer in 1936 as one of the first airline stewardesses, had always encouraged me to travel and see the world, but my protective father wanted me to settle down and marry. However, at the age of

5

16, after years of babysitting, I had announced my intention to never marry or have children, so he shouldn't have been surprised.

My mother defended my wanderlust to friends who asked, "How can you let shy, little Peggy go to South America of all places?" But when we were alone she proudly confided, "You're a quiet rebel," a description that made me laugh. Me? A revolutionary? Travel and adventure appealed to me because it opened the door to exploring other cultures and offered a way to escape what society expected, and I embraced it.

In September, I reported for the final leg of training at Peace Corps Headquarters in Washington, DC. All but four of the women returned, and we stayed at the Mayflower Hotel where Sandy and I were roommates again. Every day, we learned how Peace Corps/ Washington functioned and what our responsibilities would be at our posts, plus we met with the desk representatives for our respective countries.

I immediately offended the desk representative for Bolivia when I referred to the Aymara and Quechua Indians of that country as "Indians." "NEVER use that word again," she gasped, as though I had violated a universal taboo. "The proper word is c*ampesino*," she sniffed. (C*ampesino* means peasant.) Her condescending attitude continued for two weeks, and I had no choice but to tolerate it.

Nevertheless, everyone else at Peace Corps Headquarters was friendly. On our way to lunch one day, a bunch of us stepped into the elevator, and a very handsome man standing inside and chatting with a colleague smiled at us. He looked familiar. "Oh my god," we whispered as we recognized him. It was Sargent Shriver, the Peace Corps Director.

Before leaving Washington, D.C., our group lined up in front of Peace Corps Headquarters for a photo to accompany a Peace Corps newsletter article titled "You're a Volunteer WHAT?" about the new program for Volunteer secretaries and the confusion our status caused when people assumed we were well-paid State Department office staff instead.

Peace Corps Volunteer secretaries in front of Peace Corps Headquarters, Washington, D.C., September 1965. I'm in the bottom picture, sixth from the right in a white top and dark skirt. Sandy is in the same picture at the far right.

My schedule in Washington, DC allowed for some free time, so a boyfriend from New York City came to see me. Dave was a tall, handsome, charming playboy, and we spent a romantic evening in our nation's capital, but that mood changed at midnight when Dave put my Peace Corps status in jeopardy.

From the lobby, Dave phoned a friend he planned to stay with, but his friend never answered, so Dave asked if he could stay with me instead. He put me in a terrible position, torn between my affection for him and my fear of being caught by Peace Corps officials. This was 1965, years before the sexual revolution made co-ed sleeping arrangements acceptable.

Nevertheless, I brought Dave up to my room and asked Sandy, who was already in bed, if Dave could sleep on the floor. "Okay," she mumbled, "but no funny business." I threw a pillow on the floor, and Dave spent an uncomfortable night on the carpet tossing and turning. I slept fitfully, too, worried about the consequences of smuggling a man into my room. If discovered, I could have been dismissed. As Dave left the next morning, I cautioned him to make sure no one was in the hallway. I doubt if he ever had a friend in Washington, DC. After working so hard all summer, I had foolishly risked losing everything.

However, these concerns were soon forgotten in the excitement of saying goodbye to my Peace Corps friends and flying to South America. Since Maryann and I were both assigned to Bolivia, we flew there together. I wasn't scared at all. As the saying goes, "Ignorance is bliss," and I felt fearless and invulnerable.

8

CHAPTER TWO
THE ADVENTURE BEGINS

 Bolivia (in black) is a landlocked, South American country surrounded by Brazil, Paraguay, Argentina, Chile, and Peru.

It was September 24, 1965, a sunny Friday afternoon, when Maryann and I stepped off a jet airplane into the cold, thin air of La Paz, Bolivia. We had landed at the highest airport in the world on Bolivia's *altiplano,* a harsh, flat, treeless plateau 13,000 feet above sea level.

As we descended the stairway ramp to the ground, hordes of indigenous Aymara Indian boys in faded clothing and worn-out shoes, surrounded us, shouting in Spanish and fiercely competing to carry our luggage. But I couldn't understand a word; I had forgotten all my Spanish. In despair, I abandoned Maryann and pushed through the confusion into the small airport terminal furnished with benches and ticket counters, but some of the boys followed, clawing for my attention.

Amid the chaos, passengers were negotiating with taxi drivers, trying to bargain down the price of the one-hour drive into the city. First-time arrivals often paid 100 times the actual price. But we escaped this initiation rite by riding with Peace Corps personnel in their van.

Our driver was Mickey, an Assistant Peace Corps Director, whose handsome young face had recently graced the cover of the Peace Corps newsletter. I barely suppressed delight when I mentioned I had seen that picture, but Mickey looked at his young bride, who had accompanied him, and just rolled his eyes. He loaded our luggage into the van and continuously flirted with his adoring wife, paying no attention to us, as we crept along the twisting, narrow, mountain road down 1,000 feet into the bowl-shaped city, the highest capital in the world.

Our descent into La Paz, a city nestled in the majestic Andes Mountains, was breathtaking, and I stared out the window taking it all in. The brown, dry landscape was brightened only by the snow-capped peaks of the mountains surrounding the city. Along the road, I saw native Aymara Indian men in *llama* wool ponchos and colorful Andean knit wool hats with ear flaps, wearing sandals made of recycled tires. These slim, strong men carried on their backs enormous bundles four times as tall as they were.

Native Aymara Indian women, their hair braided in two, wore derby hats, shawls, and several layers of sweaters and skirts. Some carried babies on their backs wrapped in large *aguayos* (woven wool cloths featuring bright, multi-colored stripes) that tied in front; while others sat by the road selling oranges neatly stacked in small piles.

Only the main road on which we traveled was paved. Open sewers ran down dirt-covered side streets where skinny dogs and round-faced children wandered among the crowded, one-story, adobe brick dwellings.

However, that picture gradually changed as we descended further into the busy city. Modern, multi-storied buildings lined the paved, main boulevard known as the Prado. Park benches on a beautifully landscaped sidewalk in the middle of the Prado invited pedestrians to relax, while traffic lights regulated the movement of vehicles and pedestrians on the street.

Men in business suits, women in dresses, and children in white school uniforms hurried along the sidewalks on both sides of the Prado. Aggravated taxi drivers honked their horns, and exhaust fumes mixed with the faint odor of urine in the air. Tiny crowded public buses belched clouds of smoke. And at a sidewalk café, shoeshine boys pestered customers who were inspecting an alpaca rug that an indigenous street vendor had rolled out.

Most fascinating were the local people -- Aymara and Quechua Indians (*campesinos*) in traditional clothing, Caucasian Bolivians of European ancestry, and mestizos of mixed European and Indian blood. Everything was wonderfully different.

Mickey deposited Maryann and me at the modest, multi-storied Hotel La Paz near the Prado, and we were on our own. I was 23 years old, and this was my first overseas adventure.

CHAPTER THREE
THE LA PAZ OFFICE

Peace Corps Bolivia had offices in three cities - La Paz, Cochabamba and Santa Cruz (located left to right across the center of the map of Bolivia).

During our first few days in this 2½-mile-high city, Maryann and I shared a room at the Hotel La Paz. I remember gazing out the window that first night at the bright stars that appeared so low I could almost touch them. Our modest hotel provided such luxuries as heat and hot running water, comforts I would live without during my two years in Bolivia. But the loss of these comforts was minor compared to the greatest adjustment of all -- living at 12,000 feet above sea level. The high altitude affected every aspect of our lives.

The next morning, Maryann and I tested our Spanish fluency by ordering breakfast in the hotel restaurant. We felt confident when the waiter nodded his head as he took our order. However, when we were served bottles of Fanta carbonated orange soda instead of *jugo de naranja* (orange juice), we were too intimidated to complain, so we justified our lack of assertiveness by remembering the Peace Corps mantra: If it comes in a bottle, it's safe to drink.

Following breakfast, we took a taxi to the Peace Corps office housed in an attractive pale yellow, two-story residence near the main boulevard. When I opened the front door, the beautiful sunlit entry highlighted the polished wood floors, and a curved staircase to the second floor gave the space an elegant air. Perhaps this had once been the home of a wealthy family. The young female receptionist, a Bolivian national, greeted us in English and directed us upstairs. But after climbing the long stairway to the second floor office of Al Purcell, the Peace Corps Director for Bolivia, we were gasping for air.

While catching our breath, we exchanged pleasantries with Mr. Purcell, a towering, middle-aged, quiet-mannered man, who ended our brief meeting by inviting us to his home for dinner that evening. When I met his pregnant wife later that day, she was breathing heavily and suffering from exhaustion and nausea due to her delicate condition and the high altitude. I was relieved to see she had the help of a young, live-in, *campesina* woman who prepared the delicious meal. A week later, Mrs. Purcell flew back to the states to complete her pregnancy and returned to Bolivia only after the baby was born.

Maryann and I had assumed we'd be working together, but the next morning the Director assigned me to the La Paz office and Maryann to the regional office in Santa Cruz, a semi-tropical city in the eastern lowlands of the country. Cochabamba, a city in the middle of the country at 8,600 feet above sea level, was home to a third regional office. These Peace Corps offices handled administrative matters and provided the Volunteers with program and medical support.

Maryann flew to Santa Cruz, and I settled into the La Paz office which had a large staff -- five local Bolivians, seven U.S. government service professionals, and a Peace Corps Volunteer secretary named Mary, a feisty, no-nonsense young woman from Kansas City. Mary wore her short, brown hair in an attractive bob and had a confident swagger and boldness about her. Since she had already been in-country for a few months, she knew her way around.

Mary worked on the first floor with the Bolivian employees and was fearless about speaking Spanish, so her fluency was always better than mine. I was assigned to the second floor to assist the office manager, Carolyn, a beautiful blonde who spoke fluent Spanish and looked like Grace Kelly. Together, Carolyn and I worked with the Director, two Assistant Directors, and the Peace Corps doctor

The well-paid, U.S. State Department employees enjoyed an overseas hardship bonus, housing benefits, and live-in domestic help. Their standard of living was much higher than Mary's and mine, but we didn't envy them. We felt special to be Peace Corps Volunteers and expected to live as the local people did in order to blend in and work with them. Our daily expenses were relatively low, and the $100 per month living allowance covered all our basic needs.

CHAPTER FOUR
SETTLING IN

Mary suggested I rent a room from the young Bolivian couple with whom she lived in a roomy, two-story, middle-class home with polished, dark wood floors and surrounded by a handsome, black wrought-iron fence. They agreed to rent me a room and provide three meals a day for $50 a month. The couple's four-year old daughter, Dorita, and a mysterious brother-in-law named Carlos also lived there.

Mary and I had separate bedrooms across the hall from each other. My room was furnished with a comfortable bed, a nightstand, and an armoire for my clothing. But strangely, the bedroom door had a small window covered by a transparent curtain which allowed anyone, usually Carlos, to pass through the hall and look into my room. As a result, I had to stand in a corner hidden from view when I dressed.

The Bolivian couple and Carlos kept to themselves, politely greeting us when we passed each other in the hallway but rarely conversing with us. However, we did become friendly with another member of the household.

As was the custom among middle-class Bolivian families, an Aymara Indian maid, who cleaned and cooked, lived in the house. Her name was Juanita, a sweet, shy young woman, who wore her hair in two braids and dressed in traditional *campesina* clothing.

15

She served Mary and me breakfast in our respective bedrooms every morning and lunch and dinner at a small table near the kitchen where we chatted with Juanita while we ate. The family dined separately from us.

One Sunday evening, we had a glimpse into Juanita's private life, a side of her we hadn't imagined, because she always seemed to be there. She had the night off and was leaving for a date with her boyfriend. While Mary and I ate dinner, Juanita showed us a silky, new, fringed shawl she'd bought to wear with her derby hat and several layers of blouses and skirts. She couldn't wait to show it her boyfriend. As she left the house, Mary and I complimented her on how pretty she looked, but her wide grin told us she already knew.

In a poncho I bought from a street vendor, I pose with Juanita who is wearing a new shawl for a date with her boyfriend. October 1965

Juanita was a wonderful cook, and her meals were delicious, but we had to be careful about what we ate. Peace Corps training had taught us that uncooked food (such as salads) must first soak in an iodine solution for 20 minutes or be washed with boiled and filtered water. However, Bolivians didn't follow these practices, so to be safe, we ate only hot, cooked food and skipped the salads.

The challenge of living at a high altitude was compounded by the steep angle of the streets of La Paz, earning the city the title "The San Francisco of South America." And, like San Francisco, vehicles could not scale the steepest streets. Our house was at the top of such a street. To get to the house, I often rode in taxis, because it cost only 1,000 Bolivianos (8 cents) to go anywhere in the city. However, taxis could not deliver me to my front door and left me at the bottom of the hill to fend for myself.

I lived at the top of this street that taxis could not climb. La Paz, October 1965.

One evening, my taxi driver was determined to reach the top even though I had warned him it was impossible. He was sure he could do it, and I almost believed him. As the taxi started to ascend, I held my breath, but halfway up the hill, the motor sputtered and groaned, the car stalled, and we coasted backwards in silence. Not one to give up easily, the driver restarted the car and tried again, but after we rolled back a second time, he shrugged his shoulders, and I reluctantly got out of the taxi.

As I stood at the bottom of the hill, looking up, I dreaded the climb. Walking up the street on the shiny stone sidewalk was precarious. The angle was so steep that I sometimes slipped and had to steady myself by grabbing onto the wall of a building.

One evening, as I was huffing and puffing my way up the hill, I noticed a *campesina* woman across the street from me climbing the same hill, but she wasn't struggling at all. She was walking at a slow and deliberate pace, almost in slow motion, so I slowed down, too. The high altitude didn't seem to faze the indigenous people who, over the centuries, have developed a larger than average lung capacity and extra red blood cells.

For me, however, climbing that hill always left my heart racing and my lungs starved for oxygen. As soon as I reached home, I collapsed on my bed until I could breathe normally. How was I ever going to survive this ordeal for two years? Luckily, after a month, Mary and I learned of a little-known, round-about route to our house which we directed taxis to follow, and we never had to climb that hill again.

One afternoon, we attended a *fútbol* (soccer) match between La Paz and a team from a lower elevation. We empathized with the exhausted, visiting players who spent most of their time on the field bent over and gasping for air. At the same time, we laughed as the La Paz team, whose players were well adapted to the high altitude, effortlessly cruised past their opponents to score several goals. We couldn't help but cheer the home team to an easy victory. *Viva La Paz!*

CHAPTER FIVE
LA PAZ CALLING SANTA CRUZ

"La Paz -- Santa Cruz. La Paz calling Santa Cruz. Come in Santa Cruz. Over."

Each weekday at 8:30am, Mary and I crowded into a tiny room in the Peace Corps office to warm up the shortwave radio and call the Santa Cruz and Cochabamba Peace Corps offices for messages. Long-distance telephone communication in Bolivia was difficult to arrange, but the radio allowed us to quickly communicate with our offices. A Peace Corps Volunteer, an engineer named Jerry, set up and maintained the radio and taught Mary and me how to operate the bulky contraption with dozens of thick black dials and switches. It was a challenge that took us into the wilds of Bolivia.

One of those wild places was the Beni, a large tropical wilderness of swamps and forests in the northeastern part of Bolivia in the Amazon basin.

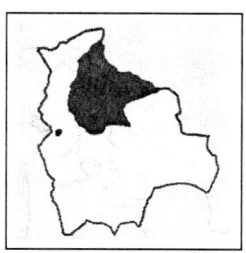

In this map of Bolivia, the Beni region is highlighted in black. The black dot on the left represents La Paz.

Since there were no roads into the Beni, it was accessible only by airplane, horseback, or boat.

Peace Corps Volunteers assigned to that region lived in isolated villages, and the best way to reach our office was to leave a message with José, a shortwave radio operator in the Beni, who communicated with us every weekday morning.

After talking with the Santa Cruz and Cochabamba offices, Mary and I waited for the appointed time of 8:45am, listening to the high-pitched squeaks and squeals in the airwaves until we heard José's distant voice calling, "*Buenos días, La Paz*" (Good morning, La Paz). Since José spoke no English, we spoke with him in Spanish, saying "*Cambio*" (Change) instead of "Over" when we switched the transmission back and forth as we took turns speaking.

Mary and I handled this task together, because the messages could be a matter of life and death. Mary's Spanish was better than mine, so she took the lead when José was on the line. Unfortunately, the crackling static and a frequency that faded in and out plus José's rapid speech made it almost impossible to understand him. My stomach was in knots every morning when we called José. This was Spanish under fire! Our favorite message from him was always, *"No hay nada."* ("There's nothing."). When we heard those words, Mary and I exchanged relieved glances as we signed off.

The most dramatic exchange occurred one morning when José skipped the usual small talk and immediately launched into a message full of unfamiliar Spanish words. The more we asked him to slow down and repeat the message, the more agitated he became. Something serious had happened to a Peace Corps Volunteer, but we couldn't understand the entire message, so I ran to get Carolyn, my officemate, who was fluent in Spanish.

José told her a female Volunteer had been attacked by a rabid bat and needed to be transported to La Paz immediately for a series of rabies shots, but the next commercially scheduled flight out of the Beni was three days away. The matter was resolved when the Peace Corps arranged for a private plane to bring the Volunteer to La Paz where she was treated, recovered, and eventually returned to the Beni.

Many months later, the Peace Corps discontinued communication with the Beni radio operator, but I don't remember why. A modern shortwave radio the size of a breadbox replaced the antique one and operated out of a small sitting room next to my office. From then on, I alone handled the daily communication with the Santa Cruz and Cochabamba offices and left the radio on all day so I could hear them calling. I even talked with my training buddy, Maryann, in the Santa Cruz office a few times.

To make calls within the city of La Paz, we dialed the phone number directly, but long-distance service to other cities was complicated. To talk to someone in Potosí, for example, a telephone operator set up a telephone/shortwave radio hookup with the other party which took an hour to arrange, then called us back, and switched the shortwave transmission back and forth as each party took turns speaking. Since our voices had to pass through a telephone and a shortwave radio, we had to shout and do it all in Spanish. It was exhausting.

Operating the shortwave radio was one of my many responsibilities. Unlike most Volunteers who were sent to their sites with undefined assignments, Volunteer secretaries had the most structure, working five days a week from 8:30am to 6pm with an hour and a half for lunch. Mary and I worked on outside projects and were given time off to do so, but most of our day was spent in the office.

In this Polaroid photo, I'm on the telephone at Carolyn's desk. Behind me is the blackboard that lists the travel plans of Peace Corps officials in the country.
La Paz, 1965.

My desk on the second floor sat perpendicular to Carolyn's in front of a large window in a spacious but chilly room. A portable kerosene heater hovered nearby, warming our legs and hands. Other furnishings included an electric typewriter for Carolyn, a manual typewriter for me, three filing cabinets, a telephone, two credenzas, and a large blackboard listing all nine Peace Corps officials in Bolivia and their travel plans to villages where Volunteers worked on engineering, health, education, and community development programs.

I typed reports and correspondence in Spanish and English, handled telephone calls in both languages, maintained files on the Volunteers, answered numerous questions from them, and made travel arrangements for Peace Corps officials and Volunteers to the United States. A curious part of my job was assisting the male Peace Corps doctor by holding the flashlight when he administered pap smears on female Volunteers at their end-of-service medical checkouts. I felt squeamish the first time but eventually proved to be a reliable medical assistant.

CHAPTER SIX
DANCING AT 12,000 FEET
ABOVE SEA LEVEL

Among the Bolivian staff were two bilingual young women from the Bolivian aristocracy – Susana, a lively blonde who made me laugh in both languages, and Ana, a thoughtful brunette whose father had been President of Bolivia a few years earlier. They worked on the first floor for two Assistant Peace Corps Directors. Susana and Ana lived with their respective parents in the wealthy suburb of Calacoto at a more comfortable altitude 2,000 feet lower than La Paz.

One Saturday afternoon, Susana and Ana invited Mary and me to join them and twenty of their girlfriends for lunch at Susana's house. Susana picked us up at the office in her sporty little car and drove along a beautifully paved, winding road down the mountain to her elegant home.

Once there, Mary and I went around the room shaking hands with the attractive young women who were as well groomed, well dressed and well educated as Susana and Ana. They all knew each other and spoke Spanish excitedly and rapidly as girlfriends do when they get together, and I hardly understood a word. At lunchtime, two live-in *campesina* women served us a delicious meal as we sat at a long table in a room with a wall of windows showing a dramatic view of a deep ravine. This was our glimpse into how the aristocracy lived.

In addition to Susana and Ana, other Bolivian office staff included Gregorio, a short, sturdy, handsome, indigenous man who was the office messenger. He and his wife, Josefina, and two children lived in a little white stucco house behind the Peace Corps office.

Gregorio and Josefina were asked to pose for photos for a Peace Corps/Washington brochure about Bolivia's government-sponsored tuberculosis control programs in which Peace Corps Volunteers participated. I had never worked in a health program, but I, too, was asked to pose for a photo where I appear to be injecting a hypodermic needle into Josefina's arm.

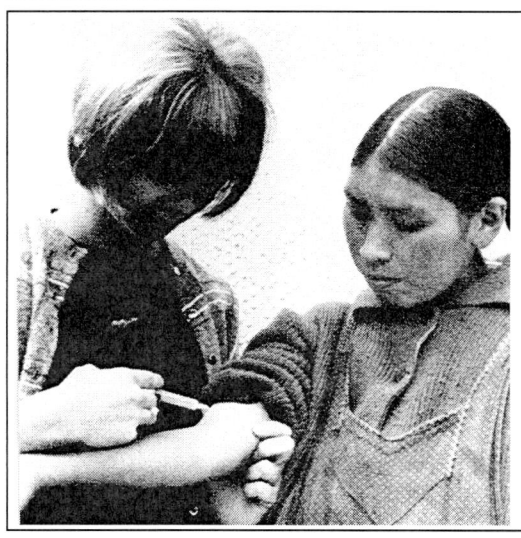

The caption for the photo was: Volunteers work in teams to locate infected persons and help treat them.

I had no idea how to hold the needle and had to be coached by the American photographer. Josefina picked up on this right away and, as she stretched out her arm, she kept a close eye on me to make sure I didn't scratch her. We look serious in the photo, but moments before, we had been laughing because it was just make-believe.

Peace Corps Volunteers passed through the main La Paz office when they arrived in-country, so I met everyone. And, because of frequent errands to the American Embassy, I knew Embassy personnel and the Marines who guarded the entrance, plus those at the U.S. Agency for International Development (USAID). We Americans in La Paz were a small community and regularly socialized at receptions at the American Ambassador's residence or at Peace Corps parties, of which there were many.

I attended one such party during my first weekend in La Paz and met most of the Volunteers stationed in the city and some who had come in from their *campo* (rural countryside) sites. Most were in their 20s, well educated with college degrees, curious about other countries and cultures, and eager to make a meaningful contribution in the world. But they were also interested in having lots of fun, and we drank and laughed and danced a lot. I dated several of the guys and learned how to dance the *cumbia* and the *wiño*, two Latin American dances.

I frequently partied with a group of Peace Corps Volunteers at the Bamboo Bar, a La Paz nightclub that featured *Los Blackbirds*, a band of four talented young men from Brazil who wore mop-top haircuts, sang in English, and played songs made famous by the Beatles who had taken America by storm just the year before. Because there were more guys than girls, Mary and I danced continuously, carried away with the popular new music and gasping for air in the high altitude. We were on the dance floor so much that the band came to recognize us and waved and smiled whenever we arrived at the club. They loved our enthusiasm for dancing to the Beatles music, and we loved them for playing it.

Although I was a Peace Corps Volunteer, I was also an office staff member, and that gave me access to confidential information other Volunteers didn't have. For example, I knew who was requesting permission to marry, who was going home for funeral or other leave, who was being reprimanded or reassigned, and who was being evacuated to Washington, DC for an abortion.

This was years before the Supreme Court decision of Roe v. Wade legalized abortion, but Peace Corps/Washington quietly got the job done. I had to pack one such Volunteer's personal belongings for shipment back to the U.S., because she had already left Bolivia and wasn't going to return. My job required discretion but it embodied the best of both worlds – the structure of the office and the freedom to explore and contribute outside that setting – and I loved it.

CHAPTER SEVEN
THE BULLFIGHT

Culture shock assaulted us every day in Bolivia, but it especially hit hard one beautiful Sunday afternoon in October when Mary and I attended our first bullfight. Elsa, a long-haired, perky young Bolivian friend of Mary's, invited us to join her for the event. When we met at her home, Elsa kissed us on both cheeks, as is the Latin custom, and escorted us to the dusty, local bullring and through the round arches of its ancient entryway.

Mary (center) with Elsa (right) and Linda (left, who lived and worked in Elsa's house). La Paz, October 1965.

"*Sol o sombra*?" (sun or shade), she asked, as we approached the ticket booth. Deferring to Elsa, our trusty guide, we bought three cheap seats in the sun and followed her down a dark, narrow corridor toward the center of the ring where I ignored a pushy vendor renting seat cushions. After exiting the hallway into the bright sunlight reflecting off the sandy arena below, we climbed up the wooden steps to our seats as a chorus of boys beneath the bleachers hooted and looked up our dresses. Gathering our skirts around our legs, we sat down on the hard, rough benches, and I immediately regretted not renting that seat cushion.

Nevertheless, I was thrilled to be at a real bullfight and breathed in the atmosphere – the cigar smoke, the blazing sun, and the roar of the crowd. The centuries-old spectacle began at exactly 3:30pm when a small brass band sitting in the shade across the arena from us bungled the first few notes of the "*paso doble,*" the traditional music that signals the start of the bullfight. Two slim young matadors, Enrique Esparza from Mexico and Miguel López Trujillano from Peru, paraded around the arena looking sexy in their tight-fitting, sparkling costumes called *trajes de luz* (suits of light). The crowd cheered as though they were movie stars.

Suddenly a furious bull exploded into the ring. The graceful movements of the matador as he waved his red cape and controlled the bull were like a ballet. In unison, the crowd rewarded each successful pass with a loud "*Ole!*" But for Mary and me, the beauty of the spectacle soon turned to horror when long spikes were plunged into the poor beast's neck and back. As the bull rocked back and forth on unsteady legs, blood from his neck dripped onto the sand, mucous flowed from his nose, feces ran down his legs, and his dusty tongue hung listlessly out of his mouth. Mary and I were horrified and started to cry, which amused those around us. Our loyal friend Elsa gamely defended us, explaining it was our first bullfight, but that only increased their laughter and our tears.

We were especially sickened when the matador failed to kill the bull with a final, clean plunge of the sword into the top of the bull's neck. The matador tried over and over again, butchering and torturing the poor creature. The angry crowd whistled its disapproval, and someone shouted "*Basura!*" (garbage). Finally, the matador's sword killed the dying beast, and the crowd cheered as the matador strutted around the ring accepting flowers and a live chicken from his fans. A green jeep leaped into the bullring and unceremoniously dragged the bull's dead carcass away, leaving behind a trail of bright red blood that arena workmen in baggy overalls quickly raked over with sand.

Aficionados do not view bullfighting as a cruel sport but instead consider it an art form in which man defeats death symbolized by the bull. However, that afternoon, we saw only the torture of an animal. We weren't so naïve as to think the bull would be spared, but we hadn't imagined the killing would be so brutal and cruel.

Distressed that there were still three more bulls to kill, Mary and I wanted to escape, but our friend Elsa was frowning and biting her lip. We couldn't bear to disappoint her nor call more attention to ourselves by leaving early, so we hunkered down until the bitter end, averting our eyes from the arena for the next hour and a half.

When the bullfight was finally over and we stood up to leave, the boys under the bleachers cheered as they looked up our dresses again. Disgusted with their adolescent behavior, we clutched our skirts around our knees, hampering our legs as we wormed our way down the wooden steps to the exit where we vowed never, ever to return. And we never did.

CHAPTER EIGHT
CULTURE SHOCK

In Bolivia, the bullfight always started on time, but nothing else did. The relaxed Latin approach to time was another culture shock. There was little pressure to be punctual. North Americans live according to schedules, but Latin Americans live a leisurely life. My first clash with this cultural difference occurred shortly after I arrived in Bolivia.

One of Mary's English-language students, a young, excitable, wild-haired, Bolivian woman named Alisa, invited us to a party one Sunday afternoon at the home she shared with her parents. According to the invitation, the party began at 4pm, so that's when we arrived. However, no one answered the door and when we started to leave, Alisa burst out of the house in a robe and curlers, yelling our names, and demanding to know why we were so early. When we pointed to the 4pm time on the invitation, she screamed, "That doesn't mean four o'clock!"

Alisa's bizarre behavior alarmed us, but we allowed her to coax us inside to a sitting room where she closed the door, isolating us from the family. The household, now roused from its *siesta*, began to stir with activity. For two hours, Mary and I huddled on the couch, contemplating our apparent breach of etiquette as we listened to the family get dressed and prepare for the party.

At 6pm, a calmer Alisa released us from the sitting room and led us down a hallway filled with the fragrant odors of cooking. In the living room, we met her gracious parents and the guests who were just arriving. As Mary and I spoke Spanish with everyone, we sampled food from the buffet spread out on a large table. However, the situation quickly deteriorated when Alisa hovered overhead, directing us to eat this and drink that, while hardly allowing any time to swallow in between bites of food and bits of conversation.

By 11pm, seven hours after our untimely arrival, the party was still going strong when we risked Alisa's wrath by telling her we had to leave. She shrieked that our "early" departure meant we hadn't had a good time, but although we reassured her otherwise, nothing calmed her. Nevertheless, we said our goodbyes and as we walked down the darkened street to the bus stop and listened to Alisa wail away in the night air, we shook our heads in disbelief. Mary was so disgusted that we never saw Alisa again.

Although this is an extreme example, cultural misunderstandings about time were frequent. When I made plans with Bolivian friends, I'd jokingly ask if they were going to arrive at *hora Americana* (American time), or *hora Boliviana* (Bolivian time). No matter the answer, *hora Boliviana* reigned supreme, and I often waited on street corners for Bolivian friends who showed up late or not at all. But apologies were never offered, because that was the Latin way.

Another culture shock made me fear for my personal safety in public places. One morning, Mary and I attended the Day of the Sea parade, an annual event at which Bolivians protested the loss of their coastline to Chile as

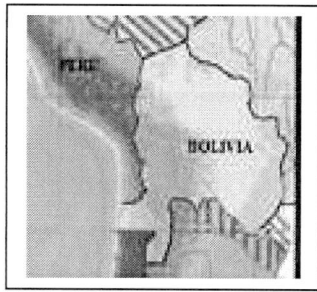

a result of the War of the Pacific (1879-1883). This 1879 map before the war shows Bolivia's narrow access to the Pacific coast. But after the war, the loss of that strip of land left Bolivia landlocked and isolated. At the parade, marchers carried small, papier-mâché boats, while others rode on parade floats with a nautical theme, all of which symbolized Bolivia's hope of regaining its seaport.

After the event, as Mary and I walked home, three restless teenage boys, riled up from the parade, followed closely behind. They taunted us and made rude comments in Spanish which we ignored, but when they touched our backs and buttocks, we could no longer ignore them. We whipped around, and as Mary lunged at the boys and shooed them away, she yelled, "*Vaya che! No nos molesten!*" (Go away! Don't bother us!) This gave them pause, and they eventually did leave us alone.

However, this wasn't an isolated incident. Mary and I were often groped by men while standing on a crowded bus, waiting to cross the street, and shopping in the marketplace. It's curious that the Spanish word to annoy or bother is *molestar* which sounds like the English word molest.

Some months later, however, I really was molested. It happened one afternoon as I walked along the Prado, the beautiful main boulevard of La Paz. Strolling past the colorful cavalcade of people on the sidewalk and surveying the panorama of outdoor cafés, hotels, shops, and office buildings, I was enjoying the sights and sounds of a vibrant city when, in a flash, everything faded. A young, dark-haired man ran up behind me and plunged his hand under my dress and between my legs. Horrified, I turned to look at him, but he flew past me and vanished into the crowd. Shocked and nauseous, I stood paralyzed while pedestrians walked around me as though nothing had happened.

From that moment on, whenever I walked along the main boulevard, I was on guard, my stomach in knots, constantly turning my head to see who was behind me, fearful and anxious about protecting myself. It was unnerving. I couldn't even wear slacks. Only dresses and skirts were acceptable attire for women.

A week later on the Prado, I saw a tall, blond Peace Corps Volunteer named Keith and told him about the sexual assault. Keith suggested I continue my walk, and he would follow half a block behind, ready to catch the perpetrator if I were assaulted again. When I reached the end of the boulevard, no one had attacked me, and I waited for Keith to catch up. However, he left me feeling even more vulnerable when he said, "Everyone I passed was talking about you."

The attack was often on my mind, but I was never assaulted again. Nevertheless, I had to face some truths. I knew my blonde hair and blue eyes meant I would never blend into a Latin culture, and I had accepted that reality when I chose to live in a foreign country away from my support system of family, friends, and American values. However, by doing so and learning a new language and customs, I often felt like a vulnerable child trying to understand how everything worked. And although I was drawn to the adventure and excitement of living in a foreign culture, I also suffered from occasional anxiety which affected my sense of identity, belonging, and safety.

CHAPTER NINE
THE BLACK MARKET

My housing situation came to a crisis after two months when the *Señora* of the house still refused to give me clean sheets. Mary and I were infuriated by this baffling decision, so we decided to move. We knew we'd miss Juanita's wonderful cooking, but we wanted the independence of our own place.

We found a little, white stucco house within walking distance of the Peace Corps office that rented for $50/month. It was located behind the main house, an attractive, large, two-story home surrounded by a high wall topped with jagged pieces of glass and owned by a middle-class Bolivian couple.

The wife was cheerful, short, and plump, and her husband had one of those pencil-thin moustaches favored by Latin men and traditionally grown as proof of Caucasian blood. (Indians cannot grow facial hair.) Their little white dog answered to the name of Pluto, and the maid was a young, plump, indigenous girl named Serafina.

Mary and I loved our new home which we scrubbed and painted as soon as we moved in. The living room was furnished with several wobbly chairs, a little bookcase, a large wooden table, and *llama* rugs. The bedroom also had *llama* rugs plus two beds, a nightstand and an armoire, while the tiny kitchen boasted a sink and an electrical two-burner hot plate.

We were allowed to use the refrigerator and telephone in the main house.

The tap water was undrinkable, so we had to boil it for 20 minutes and pour it through a tall, ceramic water filter/storage container provided by the Peace Corps. Now we could drink clean water and eat fruit and salad ingredients after washing them in the purified water.

The following weekend, we celebrated our independence by inviting three male Peace Corps Volunteers to our home for breakfast. We served them French toast, freshly squeezed orange juice, and hot cinnamon rolls baked in a square-shaped, portable, metal "oven" that sat over the hot plate.

However, two problems followed us from our former home: staying clean and staying warm. The shower in our tiny bathroom drenched the room and drained through a hole in the floor. After turning on the cold water, we switched on the electrical heating element in the showerhead which warmed the water as it sputtered out, but the heating element often short-circuited, emitting sparks and a loud POP, followed by a burning smell and ice cold water.

Afraid of being zapped, we abandoned the electrical shower and resorted to sponge baths which also proved challenging. Boiling water at 12,000 feet above sea level requires a temperature higher than 212°F, so it took forever to heat up the water.

During the day, the air temperature warmed up to the 50s, but at night it plunged into the 30s. It was cold, and houses had no central heating, so we borrowed a kerosene heater from the Peace Corps office which sat unused because we were too lazy to drag fuel home from the marketplace and skittish about the fire danger. Instead, we piled on blankets and wore layers of clothing, socks, gloves, and hats to stay warm. Nevertheless, our living conditions were relatively comfortable compared with Volunteers in the *campo* who had neither electricity nor running water.

The biggest change in our routine was preparing our own meals. There were no supermarkets in Bolivia, so we shopped in the open-air market. In spite of its name, there was nothing secretive or illegal about our favorite marketplace, *el Mercado Negro* (the Black Market). Since vendors had no

I negotiate with an indigenous female vendor in a Bolivian market.

paper bags, we piled everything into a large straw basket, quickly weighing it down until we could barely lift it.

The Black Market was a hilly maze of crowded wooden stalls bursting with everything imaginable. The male vendors wore alpaca sweaters and fedora hats, and the women, sometimes with a baby strapped to their backs, wore derby hats, shawls, and several layers of skirts and blouses.

On display were bread, fruit, vegetables, silver and tin wares, derby hats, green shampoo in tiny plastic pouches attached like sausages, wooden flutes, alpaca ponchos, *llama* rugs, toiletries, detergents, and baskets. Raw meat sat on plates as vendors playfully brushed away large flies while tantalizing odors from sizzling meat mixed with the smell of discarded fruit along an open sewer that ran down the side of the street.

I saw a beverage being prepared by a man whose bare foot stomped on fruit in a washbasin. The finished product, poured into individual glasses, sat on a little stand by his side awaiting thirsty customers.

A *campesino,* wearing a wool poncho and an Andean knit wool hat with ear flaps, carried on his back a blanket full of potatoes. He had traveled that morning on a big-wheeled open-bed truck from his rural village on the *altiplano* to sell his goods at the marketplace. Potatoes, of which there are 200 varieties, originated in Bolivia and serve as its main staple.

Bargaining was a necessary and refined art in the marketplace, one that I never felt comfortable with, but Mary played the game well. Her confident, playful demeanor charmed the vendors who enjoyed jousting with her, but I always gave in too easily, disappointing those who expected a good contest.

In addition to the marketplace, there was a tiny neighborhood shop I often stopped in on my way home from work to buy *pan* (bread) and *huevos* (eggs) for breakfast. The shop was crammed from floor to ceiling with fresh, canned, and packaged food, soap, toiletries, and bottles of soda. A narrow pathway led to where the indigenous, middle-aged, male shopkeeper sat. Hanging on a wall in a place of honor behind him was a framed picture of President John F. Kennedy. As I approached the owner, I always glanced up at the picture, basking in the knowledge that we both admired the fallen President. When I said, "*Hola, tiene huevos*?" (Do you have eggs?), he would, without any hint of disapproval, wrap up half a dozen eggs for me in a piece of newspaper. I later learned that "*Tiene huevos*" is a vulgar slang expression meaning, "Do you have balls?" and I should have said, "*Hay huevos*?" which means "Are there eggs?" I never forgot that lesson.

Because of atmospheric conditions in the high altitude, everything took longer to cook. Shopping for food and preparing meals became a full-time job, but we already had full-time jobs. After several weeks of this endless chore, we discovered the *pensión*. For only $25/month, we ate the lunch and dinner of the day, seven days a week at a neighborhood restaurant. The generous meal included an appetizer; hot homemade soup; freshly baked bread; meat, fish, or chicken; potatoes; vegetables; and dessert, usually *flan* (a syrupy custard). The *pensión* was a godsend, and we loved it.

CHAPTER TEN
TUPAC KATARI UNIVERSITY

A month after I arrived in La Paz, the Peace Corps offered me the opportunity to teach English three nights a week at Túpac Katari University. This was my chance to use the skills I had learned in Peace Corps training, so I gladly accepted. Túpac Katari University, located in the center of the city, was a public university, a less expensive alternative for students who couldn't afford a private college.

The university was named after an indigenous Bolivian leader named Túpac Katari (pictured here). In 1781 when Spain controlled La Paz, he had led a rebel Aymara Indian army that laid siege to La Paz, destroying government property and churches. Although the rebellion  failed, Túpac Katari was still revered among the indigenous people.

I first saw the university in the evening after working all day in the office. When I looked up at the skeletal framework of the building, it appeared to be either under construction or abandoned, but it was neither. As my eyes adjusted to the darkness, I saw people walking along hallways that were open to the air, and when I entered the mud-colored building, I stepped around dripping water and rain puddles as I passed dimly-lit classrooms until I found mine.

My large classroom was overflowing with 75 lively, noisy, young adult male and female students of mestizo heritage, bundled up in jackets and coats and crammed together on wooden benches attached to desks. It was cold, so I kept my coat on, too. I introduced myself to the teacher, a short, slim, thin-haired, middle-aged Bolivian gentleman dressed in a suit. We spoke in Spanish, so I had no idea how well he spoke English. He suggested I take a seat and observe the class for a while, and the students whispered among themselves as they checked me out.

The teacher ran a lively class and taught at an energetic pace, speaking what apparently was English, while the students enthusiastically repeated exactly what he said. However, his English was so heavily accented that I couldn't understand a single word. The teacher's English was incomprehensible. When he turned to speak English to me, all 75 pairs of eyes spun around to focus on my face and watch my reaction, but I still had no idea what the teacher had said. I didn't want to embarrass the poor man by saying I couldn't understand him, so I smiled and nodded my head, and that seemed to satisfy everyone.

At that point, the teacher turned the class over to me, smiled, bowed slightly, and left the room. As if a signal had been given, the room erupted into total chaos. Students shouted, laughed, wrestled, and threw paper at each other, as though school had been dismissed. To add to the disorder, curious students from other classes cracked open the door, yelled "Hello" and "Goodbye," and slammed the door shut.

I steeled myself as I stood up in front of the room, took a deep breath, and in my loudest voice demanded *"Silencio, por favor!"* (Silence, please!). But no one paid any attention except the students in the first two rows who quietly looked up at me in sympathy, desperate to learn English, but resigned to the bedlam. I had completely lost control of the class and felt a failure in my first attempt at working outside the Peace Corps office. However, I persevered, and the students eventually became accustomed to me and calmed down enough so I was able to teach them some English.

There was a textbook to guide me in my lesson plans, and I supplemented it with conversational exercises. Túpac Katari University had been open for only a year and was still quite disorganized. The administrators were so grateful to have a native speaker teaching English that they left me on my own to do whatever I wanted in the classroom. They figured I knew best. I wasn't paid a salary because I was a Peace Corps Volunteer, so the price was right.

When I arrived for class one evening, my students were more boisterous than usual and shouted over each other that classes had been cancelled for the night. Bolivian President, General Alfredo Ovando, who shared the joint military presidency with Commander of the Air Force, René Barrientos, was scheduled to speak to the student body momentarily. In their excitement, my students virtually carried me along with them to a large assembly room where the speech was to take place. The room was chilly from the cold night air, so we kept our coats on and

43

huddled together on the wooden benches, awaiting the President.

When President Ovando (pictured here), a slim, middle-aged man with a moustache, entered the room, you could have heard a pin drop. He wore a military uniform decorated with a parade of medals, and his visor hat remained firmly on his head.  Standing in front of a lectern, he gave a solemn 20-minute speech about education and patriotism to his rapt audience. To my surprise, my unruly students were quiet, attentive and respectful. I had never seen them so well behaved.

Every night after class, several of them walked me to my bus stop, competing for my attention with lots of questions. They called me Miss Peggy, which they pronounced Mēēs Peggy. "Mēēs Peggy, *de donde es usted*?" (Where are you from?), "Mēēs Peggy, *le gusta Bolivia*?" (Do you like Bolivia?), and so on. They were very curious about me, my family, and America, and I learned a lot of Spanish from them.

In letters home to my family, I affectionately referred to my students as "my 75 devils" and became friendly with many of them. After class one evening, I invited several students to my home. We listened to their records of Bolivian music and my Beatles album, and I taught them three American dances popular at the time – the frug, the jerk, and the monkey.

The semester went well until final exams, when I was shocked to see students looking in their textbooks and sharing answers. I told them to work independently and not to use their books, but they continued to do so. An exam was considered a group effort, and the students were bewildered by my disapproval.

At the end of my only semester at Túpac Katari, the students gave me a party in December 1965, complete with invitations printed on embossed linen paper, lots of food, strong drinks, and Latin music. The printed invitation, in which my last name was misspelled, translates into English as:

A Group of Friends
Has the pleasure to invite you to the Social Reception that in honor of Professor of English, Miss Peggy Dikersson, will occur on Saturday, the 11th, at 5:30 pm in the location of the
U.P.T.K.
Thank you for your kind attendance.

As the guest of honor at the party held at the university, I was expected to drink lots of alcohol and dance the *cumbia* (a popular, rhythmic, Latin American dance) all night long. If I rested for one moment to catch my breath in the high altitude, my students panicked, fearing I wasn't having a good time, refilled my glass, and whisked me onto the dance floor again. I felt as though I was in one of those Depression-era dance marathons in which couples danced until they dropped. Luckily, I had the stamina to keep going, but I was exhausted by the end of the night trying to please my students.

However, I was also very touched by their kindness and grateful for the farewell party. I realized I'd made a connection with them and, without knowing it, had met one of the Peace Corps goals – to promote a better understanding of Americans among the people of the host country. At the same time, I realized the unique opportunity and responsibility I had as my country's representative overseas.

I never again taught at Túpac Katari. Although I was scheduled to teach there in March 1966, classes never began, and I moved on to teach at other locations.

CHAPTER ELEVEN
A TRIP ON THE *ALTIPLANO*

The 13,000-foot *altiplano* (high plain) surrounding La Paz was a moonscape. There were no trees and, except for scattered tufts of scrub grass, everything was brown and dry. There was no electricity, no plumbing, no telephones, and no paved roads. Only small clumps of villages existed here and there separated by a vast emptiness, with rugged, cloud-capped mountains in the distance. The *altiplano* was lonely and cold, and the only sound was the wind. Nevertheless, the Aymara Indians have survived for centuries on this desolate, barren, high plateau. The *altiplano* is the most extensive area of high plateau in the world (except for Tibet) and extends into Bolivia, Argentina, Chile and Peru.

A sketch of a big-wheeled, open-bed transport truck on the *altiplano*.

Peace Corps Volunteers came into the La Paz office from their *altiplano* villages grimy and bedraggled, covered with dust from head to toe, and barely able to speak after traveling on big-wheeled, open-bed transport trucks, the only transportation on the *altiplano*. But after checking into the Hotel Newman for a shower and a change of clothing, they were reborn. When I saw them later at the Newman Bar, a Peace Corps hangout, they'd regale us with amusing stories about life on the *altiplano.* I was curious to see this mysterious, remote region for myself, and it wasn't long before I did.

During my first couple of months in La Paz, I dated several Bolivian young men and Peace Corps Volunteers, but by November I had fallen in love with a Volunteer named Doug, a handsome, dark blond, medium tall, young man who laughed easily and lived in an apartment around the corner from me. He worked with an older American named Dave, a well-paid, USAID employee who served as Director of the National Community Development Program. The purpose of the program was to assist *campesinos* on the *altiplano* with community development projects such as school construction and potable water systems.

Dave was a tall, slim, white-haired gentleman who lived with his wife in the wealthy suburb of Calacoto (2,000 feet lower than La Paz) in a large house graced with a winding, mahogany banister up to the second floor. Most Saturdays, Doug, his roommate, and I drove there to ride horses, play the guitar, sing folk songs, participate in spirited debates, and feast on delicious meals prepared by the household staff.

Doug was planning a five-day trip to the *altiplano* with another Peace Corps Volunteer named Ramón and a Bolivian Government Community Development Officer named Jaime. The purpose of the trip was to visit several villages, some of which had Peace Corps Volunteers, and to check on community development projects and the need for Peace Corps assistance.

Doug invited me to join them for the trip in December 1965, and I accepted. Classes had ended at Tupac Katari University, and the Peace Corps office gave me the time off. This was my chance to leave the city and see something different.

On the morning of our trip, we started the climb up the paved mountain road out of La Paz to the *altiplano* in a USAID four-wheel-drive vehicle. We were warmly dressed in sweaters, jackets, and blue jeans, including myself, although I would never wear jeans in the city. Ramón was a tall, dark, good-looking, entertaining young man who amused us with his non-stop banter, often speaking in Spanish so Jaime could understand. By contrast, Jaime, a handsome, friendly, Bolivian gentleman who drove the vehicle and spoke no English, was quiet, but he laughed just as much as we did at Ramón's humorous stories.

An hour after we started the climb, we reached El Alto (The High) Airport and the town of El Alto. Before we embarked into the wilderness, we stopped at a roadside stand to eat *salteñas*, a delicious, warm, pastry that holds a juicy, spicy combination of meat and vegetables. We ate the hand-held pastry with caution and leaned forward so the juice that inevitably spilled out onto our hands and dripped onto the ground wouldn't soil our clothing. Doug often brought *salteñas* into the Peace Corps office for me, and we'd sneak into the back kitchen to eat them.

Now fortified with our snack, we continued our trip into the *campo* on a narrow, rocky, unpaved, dirt road, passing big-wheeled, open-bed transport trucks coming into the city packed to the breaking point with *campesino* passengers, live chickens, bundles of *llama* wool, and woven reed baskets full of potatoes and vegetables. The men and women, hanging onto the slatted wood sides of the truck as they stood in the open bed, were wrapped up in shawls, sweaters, wool ponchos, knit wool hats, fedoras, and derby hats. They had ruddy complexions from the cold, windy ride, and there were no smiles on their faces.

Our first stop was Penas, a scruffy village near Lake Titicaca with several small, one-story buildings of adobe brick, a sun-baked mixture of dirt and water. We met with two Peace Corps Volunteers who lived there, Israel and Fran, and discussed their community development projects and the need for more Peace Corps assistance. I was surprised to see Fran wearing a skirt in the cold climate.

Then we headed deeper into the *campo*, rarely passing another vehicle. The rough, dirt road was deserted. Once in a while, we'd see a *campesino* tending his herd of *llamas* or carrying water. In the small villages which suddenly appeared and just as quickly disappeared, small, adobe brick houses and shops hugged both sides of the narrow road as it cut through the middle of town. Large stones piled on top of each other served as fences. Tiny windows pierced the walls of the one-story, earthen houses, and all the doors were closed. It was rare to see anyone walking around in this hostile environment. But after a while, even this seemed like modern civilization compared with what we encountered.

To reach one village, we left the road entirely to travel on a rocky, dried-up river bed. The constant bouncing and swaying were unbearable. My teeth banged against each other, and all conversation ceased because of the painfully incessant racket. My insides took a beating, and I began to wonder what I'd gotten myself into.

Of course, there were no public bathrooms in the *campo*. Since there were no trees or bushes either, it was difficult to find any privacy for the call of nature. One time, I was crouched behind a stone wall, with my companions some distance away on the other side, when out of nowhere a *campesino* appeared on a hillside. He brazenly put his hands on his hips and stared at me. It didn't help to stare back, so I quickly returned to my friends.

We visited one village that was so high above the clouds that we actually looked down on the billowy bundles of mist. At 14,000 feet above sea level, we felt as though we were at the top of the world, a world that was cold, overcast, and silent. Jaime led us to one of the small, one-story, adobe brick buildings in the village. Inside, ten *campesino* men wearing knit wool hats and sweaters were seated along a wall in a crowded room warmed by a kerosene heater. The men shyly smiled and greeted us as we went around the room shaking hands with each one. After Jaime exchanged only a few words in the Aymara language with the village leader, we shook hands with everyone all over again before leaving. It would have been rude not to do so.

The *campesino* village leader invited us to his small earthen home, and we sat on *llama* rugs around a kerosene heater while we drank glasses of hot *maté* tea served by his wife, her hair braided in two and wearing a full-length apron over her multiple skirts and sweaters. The hot glass warmed my hands as our gracious hosts spoke their Aymara language with Jaime who translated their words into Spanish for us. I felt safe and warm with our new friends and looked around the room, taking it all in as if I had been transported to another world. It was a magical moment.

But the highlight of our trip was the day and two nights we spent at a small convent in Sorata. For several days, my traveling companions had been telling me how beautiful this place was, and I was not disappointed. As we descended more than four thousand feet, we saw the sun, green trees, bright pink flowers, and the town of Sorata nestled in a valley surrounded by spectacular 21,000-foot mountains. Suddenly, in the middle of nowhere, as if in a mirage, a lovely, white-washed stucco Spanish-style convent appeared, and we were in Shangri-La.

At a convent in Sorata, I pose with: (L-R) Ramón, two nuns, Brother Leo, and Doug on the far right. December 1965

Our welcoming American hosts were three Catholic missionaries -- a monk named Brother Leo and two nuns -- all in their 30s, he wearing the long, traditional monk's cassock and the women wearing the nun's habit. They knew Doug and Ramón from previous visits and greeted them as though they were family.

The convent had glazed tile floors, polished wood beams, curved archways, wrought iron accents, linen tablecloths, and an inner courtyard. There were no other nuns or monks there, and no need for Peace Corps assistance. This stop was purely for fun. We all helped prepare meals in the kitchen where we shared stories and laughed, and the food was delicious, especially after the typical *campo* diet we had been eating of black potatoes (a type of potato) and *llama* meat.

Since there was no electricity, we used candles at night, and everyone retired early. But instead of going to sleep, I crept up a back staircase to a balcony where I met Doug. We snuggled together on a loveseat under the stars and looked out into the pitch black darkness that surrounded us for miles around. It was blissfully quiet. We felt mischievous for meeting secretly in a convent, but this was our last stop, and we wanted to be together a little longer and enjoy the peacefulness of this beautiful place.

Our restful stay in Sorata was in sharp contrast to our rough trip on the *altiplano*, and we didn't want it to end. But soon it was time to say goodbye to our kind hosts and drive back up the mountain to the *altiplano* for our rocky, dusty, four-hour trip to La Paz. Once in the city, the noisy traffic, exhaust fumes, fast pace, and crowded streets yanked us back into civilization, and the *altiplano* was just a memory.

CHAPTER TWELVE
THE ABCs OF LITERACY

My classes at Tupac Katari University ended in December 1965, so my evenings were free until March when classes at another university were to begin. I was looking for a fresh challenge, when a La Paz Volunteer named Virginia, a young, long-haired blonde, who spoke excellent Spanish, stopped by the office and told me about her latest project. She lived in Villa Victoria, a working-class neighborhood near the mountain road to the airport, where she taught Spanish literacy to *campesino* men and women who had moved into the city from the *altiplano.*

The official language of Bolivia is Spanish, but 50 percent of Bolivians are of indigenous heritage and speak Aymara or Quechua, which are the most commonly spoken first languages in the country. When *campesinos* move into the city, they learn to speak Spanish but cannot read or write it.

In January 1966, inspired by Virginia's enthusiasm, my roommate, Mary, and I joined her in teaching Spanish literacy. Two evenings a week, after working in the office, we traveled by bus half an hour up to Villa Victoria where we arrived as the sun was setting.

Classes were held in a one-story, adobe brick dwelling in a small room with three wooden tables and benches and two hanging light bulbs. The five female, middle-aged *campesina* students, their hair in braids and bundled up in multiple skirts, sweaters, shawls, and derby hats, shyly smiled as they met us. I was a little intimidated at first because they spoke Spanish better than I, but at least I could read and write it.

Mary and I sat with the students as Virginia taught the class. She pronounced and pointed to the letters of the Spanish alphabet written on a large, white poster board that rested on an easel at the front of the room, and the students repeated what she said.

Above each letter was a hand-drawn picture of a Spanish noun that began with that letter. For example, above the letter A was a picture of a bird (*ave*), above the letter B was a picture of a baby *(bebé)*, above the letter C was a picture of a horse (*caballo*), and so on. The students learned to associate the sound of each letter by looking at the picture above it. The Spanish alphabet has the same letters as the English alphabet with the exception of W (found only in foreign words such as whiskey) and the addition of Ñ, CH, LL and RR.

We then broke up into small groups, each of us working with one or two students as they read simple Spanish words and referred to the chart. The students were serious and motivated and improved each week, and as a bonus, my Spanish also improved.

After participating in the literacy program for a month, I flew to the city of Cochabamba to give a 45-minute speech about it at a conference of Peace Corps Volunteers. I flew there on Bolivia's national airline,

Lloyd Aereo Boliviano (LAB) which was an adventure in itself.

LAB airplanes were propeller-driven DC-3s which the U.S. had unloaded in Bolivia after WWII. DC-3 cabins were not pressurized, and the planes had an  operating altitude of 10,000 feet. Nevertheless, DC-3s departed and arrived daily at the 13,000-foot-high La Paz airport, which was 3,000 feet higher than the operating altitude of the airplane. Because of the high altitude, the La Paz airport had one of the longest runways in the world. Thin air at high elevations exerts less uplift force on the airplane's wings, and, therefore, more speed and a longer runway are required for takeoff.

At boarding time, I trekked across the oily tarmac with other passengers and climbed up the stairway ramp to the airplane which was resting at an angle on its large front wheels and small back wheel. Once inside, I walked up an incline to a well-worn seat and strapped myself in. The plane started to move down the runway, and I looked out the window as it picked up speed. The runway flew by as our velocity increased. We continued coasting for an endless amount of time, but still the plane didn't lift off. I held my breath, and just as the runway ended, the ground beneath us receded, and we were finally airborne.

My flight that day was on a "meat plane." The cargo consisted of crates of live chickens stacked up behind the last row of seats at the rear of the plane. During the flight, the birds clucked noisily and fluttered their wings, sending a few wisps of plumage and a slight barnyard odor into the air. To add to the discomfort, my seat was not adjustable and the flight was bumpy. I wondered how the chickens had fared, because by the time we arrived in Cochabamba, they were eerily quiet, and I wondered if they were dead.

But the rough trip was worth it to get to Cochabama, which we called "the promised land." The second largest city in Bolivia, in the center of the country, was oxygen-rich at 8,600 feet above sea level and blessed with a warm climate, leafy green parks, and paved, flat roads throughout the city. The several-storied buildings of medium height were framed by mountains in the distance, and the traffic on the streets moved at a leisurely pace.

The Volunteers who attended the conference had arrived in Bolivia a year earlier and been assigned to villages throughout the country to work on community development projects. After a year in-country, they were reuniting to share successes and failures. One of the successes I presented was the literacy program. This was a project Volunteers could easily take back to their villages and teach.

In my role as a Peace Corps secretary, I also took notes at the conference. I had the chance to meet Volunteers from all over the country. I knew their names from my work in the office, and now I had faces to go with those names. During our free time, we had fun playing guitar, singing, dancing, swimming, sun-tanning, and riding bikes all over town.

Two days later, I flew back to La Paz to take notes at another conference of Volunteers who were reuniting for their one-year anniversary, and I gave the same 45-minute speech about the literacy program. I already knew some of the Volunteers and met several more. Since the Volunteer secretaries I trained with in Arizona were scattered throughout Latin America, I never had a one-year reunion with my group. Instead I was unofficially included with this one which had arrived in-country a few months before I had.

A couple of days later when the conference ended, we were invited to the home of U.S. Ambassador Henderson, a distinguished white-haired gentleman, and his attractive wife for champagne and hors d'oeuvres. Their beautiful residence, within walking distance of my home and the Peace Corps office, was a white, two-story, wooden, colonial-style house with pillars along the front porch. Invitations to the Ambassador's home were always a treat because of the tasteful furnishings and delicious hors d'oeuvres served by waiters who circulated among the guests.

For a couple of hours, we chatted with the Ambassador and his wife, personnel from the American Embassy, USAID employees, and other Peace Corps Volunteers. Since it was Friday, and I didn't have to work the next day, I joined a group of Volunteers that took off for the Bamboo Bar and danced into the night to the music of *Los Blackbirds*. I enjoyed my week of freedom away from the office. Even my boyfriend, Doug, was out of town.

CHAPTER THIRTEEN
CARNAVAL IN ORURO

Before the Catholic observance of Lent every year, thousands of costumed dancers and bands marched through the streets of Oruro during *Carnaval* (Carnival), the biggest annual cultural event in Bolivia.

Colorful sequins, beads, jewels, mirrors, semi-precious stones, fringe, and feathers decorated their richly ornate costumes. But the symbol of the parade belonged to the Devil Dancers (pictured here) who wore red capes,

Devil Dancers in Oruro.

heavy, jewel-encrusted tunics, and grotesque, long-horned, papier-mâche masks.

Rio de Janeiro's *Carnaval* is the most famous in the world, but *Carnaval* in Oruro, a Bolivian mining town at 12,000 feet above sea level, is the second most famous. The holiday is celebrated all over Latin America with each country celebrating in its own way. Latinos are passionate about *Carnaval*, which is a time of abandon, a time to forget one's troubles, and a time to lose oneself in the exciting revelry.

As early as January 1, 1966, as if they couldn't wait for the holiday to begin, brass bands all over La Paz began to practice the music of *Carnaval*. I got caught up in the excitement and wanted to see the famous parade in Oruro, but all the bus, train, and plane tickets were sold out, and the hotels were booked. Several Peace Corps Volunteers also wanted to see the parade, so I suggested we rent a bus and travel together.

I collected money from 25 fellow Volunteers, and my boyfriend, Doug, negotiated with a bus operator. In Oruro, a Volunteer named Brian arranged for us to stay at a house that was under construction, and if we brought sleeping bags, we could sleep in one of the completed rooms. In my excitement, I told my officemate, Carolyn, of our plans, but she frowned, shook her head, and whispered, "Good luck." I dared not ask why. It was too late for that.

On Friday evening, February 18, 1966, the night of our departure, 25 Volunteers and I were standing outside the Peace Corps office with our sleeping bags, waiting for the bus that Doug and the driver were bringing to us. Doug was late, and it was already dark.

Suddenly, out of the night came flying down the street the most rickety, beat-up, rusty, tin-can of a bus. It looked like a giant can opener had carved open two gaping holes for doors. I could see Doug standing behind the driver and looking out at us with a worried expression. How could he accept this rattle-trap? What was he thinking? When he jumped out of the bus, I peppered him with questions, but he barked back that he'd just spent half an hour arguing with the driver, and I should be pleased that sheets of aluminum had been found to place over the doors.

My Peace Corps friends gamely piled onto the tiny bus and into the surprisingly small, childlike seats. There wasn't enough legroom between the rows for a 6'2" young man named Peter, so he good-naturedly stretched out in the aisle. The driver, Jorge, a short, sturdy, middle-aged man of indigenous heritage, cheerfully greeted us, oblivious of the poor condition of his bus. His teenage son, Paco, who accompanied him, hammered sheets of aluminum over the door openings, and we started the hour-long climb out of the city up to the *altiplano*.

Once there, we left the paved road and embarked on the unpaved, unlit, dirt road to Oruro, a rocky, dusty, 145-mile ride that took six grueling hours. It felt like a trip into one of those black holes in the universe that sucks up all the light. The headlights of the bus provided the only illumination on the deserted, ill-marked *altiplano* road that had been scratched out of the earth. Occasionally, we passed some earthen dwellings, but mostly we drove through a black, windswept wilderness. The incessant rattling of the bus and loud flapping of the aluminum sheets over the doors permitted no sleep and little conversation.

At 3am, we finally arrived in the chilly, quiet streets of Oruro at Brian's house. We woke him up, and he led us through a construction area to a large, empty room where all of us unrolled our sleeping bags on the dusty concrete floor and got some sleep.

The next day was bright and sunny, and we took turns in the courtyard brushing our teeth and washing our faces at the large laundry sink that dispensed ice cold water. After breakfast at a nearby restaurant, Doug and I set out to explore Oruro, a medium-sized town alive now with tourists from all over the world.

As the parade started, we joined the large crowds six deep lining the parade route. I felt a trickle of liquid run down the back of my leg, and when I turned around, a little boy was relieving himself on my leg while his mother proudly watched. But I was not surprised. The streets of La Paz and other cities often reeked of urine. There were no public restrooms, and it was not unusual to see men, women, and children urinate in the streets.

We were encouraged to stand up front for a good view. As male dancers wearing white bear costumes and masks with bulging eyes paraded by, they chose women, mostly *gringas* (foreigners) including me, to dance with and playfully smack on the butt.

A dancer in a bear costume danced with me in the *Carnaval* parade in Oruro, February 1966.

The traditional *Carnaval* music of drum beats, wooden Andean flutes, cymbals, and brass trumpets continued throughout the day as elaborate costumes and masks flew by in flashes of color. The festival, which is descended from the ancient Andean people, is a blend of very old pagan beliefs and Christian symbols. The dancers' costumes depicted archangels, devils, Incas, black slaves, and Spanish conquistadors from Bolivian folk stories.

Water attacks, which are part of the tradition of *Carnaval*, were a constant irritant during our visit. Gangs of young Bolivian men with squirt guns and water balloons prowled the streets attacking everyone, especially *gringos*. We got more than our fair share, and Doug blamed my long blonde hair. He had never gotten so wet before.

On the following day, Sunday, a *Carnaval* guide invited us to the second floor of a building where we viewed the parade from our own window. We were offered free beer, confetti and streamers, and an explanation of the parade's festivities. Best of all, we were safe from the water balloons.

As we watched, dozens of groups totaling thousands of participants performed on foot, dancing, gyrating, jumping, twirling, and singing. Each dance group, accompanied by its own marching band, was tightly choreographed with everyone moving in unison. Besides the artistry of the dancers, it was extraordinary to witness the physical energy and stamina of the performers who danced continuously for eight hours at 12,000 feet above sea level. The parade was the most spectacular one I have ever seen, and I loved it.

On Monday morning, the day of our departure, Doug and I were heading back to the house after breakfast when we saw a pickup truck full of men throwing water balloons. We ducked around the corner to avoid them but encountered another pickup truck full of men throwing water balloons. When they saw me, it wasn't enough to just throw a balloon.

One young man leaped off the truck and came right for me. I hid behind Doug who promptly ran away. The man grabbed me, yanked back the neck of my sweater, and threw a water balloon down my back with all his might. The violent attack soaked me to the skin, and I stood there sobbing while the men in the truck laughed and drove away. When Doug returned, even he was laughing as he tried to comfort me.

Back at the house, I changed into some of Doug's clothes, because all of mine were wet. Then we joined the other Peace Corps Volunteers waiting outside. When we saw our lively little bus chugging down the street, everyone cheered. We piled aboard, and Jorge warmly greeted us as though we were old friends. Paco nailed the aluminum sheets over the door openings, and we were on our way back to La Paz. The six-hour, daylight bus ride across the *altiplano* proceeded smoothly. Our trusty, old workhorse of a bus never let us down but loyally kept plodding along and delivered us to La Paz that afternoon safe and sound.

CHAPTER FOURTEEN
TEACHING IN EL ALTO

One sunny afternoon in March 1966, I was riding a crowded public bus up the mountain to El Alto (The High), a town near the airport. I was running late, because I'd had trouble finding the *expresso* (express), but I was grateful to have an aisle seat for the hour-long trip.

However, the heavy, middle-aged *campesina* woman next to me was behaving strangely. She was madly rustling under her shawl, and when I pulled my purse away, she had already opened it. Although my wallet was still there, I was furious and shaking inside and snapped at her, "*Ladrón, ladrón, ladrón.*" (Thief, thief, thief.) Nevertheless, the woman blithely ignored me and sat there in her derby hat looking out the window for the rest of the trip.

When the bus reached the top of the mountain, it lumbered onto a wide dirt road into El Alto, a working-class suburb of La Paz, where it stopped. From here, the bus would shortly return to the city below. El Alto is a stopping-off point for *campesinos* relocating from the *campo* to the city, and many settle here.

On both sides of the nearly empty road I saw plain adobe brick, one-story dwellings, but one white building stood out. It was an attractive, two-story structure surrounded by a high, white wall topped with terra-cotta tiles. This was the Church of the

Nazarene, and I was here to teach English in its elementary school. I had volunteered when the church asked the Peace Corps for an English teacher.

As I pushed open the heavy, rust-colored iron gates into the empty, dirt courtyard, I saw to my left a plain one-story schoolhouse with four small rooms. One of the young Bolivian teachers, dressed in a skirt and sweater, warmly greeted me and introduced me to my class of second and third graders as "*Señorita Peggy, la profesora de Inglés*" (the English teacher). Thirty *campesino* boys and girls wearing white smock school uniforms over their clothes stood up from their desks and clapped their hands to welcome me. All the little girls wore their hair in two braids, as is the traditional indigenous style, and the little boys' hair was neatly trimmed.

The classroom had a blackboard, and the painted white walls were decorated with pictures of historic Bolivian heroes and Biblical Spanish verses, one of which read "*LA SANGRE DE JESUCRISTO SU HIJO NOS LIMPIA DE TODO PECADO*" (The Blood of Jesus Christ His Son Cleanses Us of All Sin.) The Church of the Nazarene was active in missionary work and had found a need here and a place to spread its message.

As I spoke with the children, I translated their names into English which made them laugh. And when I taught them simple, conversational dialogues, they enthusiastically repeated the sentences after me. Individual students performed the dialogues in front of the room, shyly giggling as they spoke the foreign-sounding words and rushing back to their seats. At the end of class, the students stood up again and clapped their hands to thank me. That afternoon I also taught the fourth and fifth graders, but because I was late, I wouldn't meet the kindergarteners and first graders until next time.

For this photo, I sat among my students at the elementary school in El Alto. March 1966.

During recess, I sat outside and watched the children play in front of the school on the treeless, sparsely traveled main road. There was no playground equipment, so the boys pretended to be angry bulls, pointing their index fingers above their heads for horns and pawing the ground with their feet, while other boys were matadors, waving imaginary capes as the "bulls" charged. The girls pretended to be mothers holding imaginary babies in their arms, rocking back and forth to comfort the "infants," and imitating the sound of babies crying, "*Wa, Wa, Wa.*"

I also had time during recess to talk with the teachers, a group of young Bolivian women, none of whom had finished high school. The Nazarene Church could not afford to pay them much, but they were devoted to the children and were working toward their diplomas and teaching certificates. Since there were no formal bathroom facilities, only the area behind the building, I drank nothing at lunch on the days I went to El Alto. Nevertheless, at the end of the afternoon, my bladder was always uncomfortably full as I rode the bouncing bus for an hour back down into the city.

For the next eight months, from March to October 1966, I traveled to El Alto two afternoons a week and taught English from 2pm to 4:30pm to four classes of students, ranging in age from five to ten. Since the unheated classrooms were cold, I kept my coat on. The altitude of the school was 1,000 feet higher than the city below, and the lack of oxygen plus wearing a heavy coat made me dizzy, and I fainted once. The children fell silent, and a teacher brought me a glass of water, but I remembered my Peace Corps training to avoid drinking water that hadn't been boiled and filtered, so I only pretended to take a sip.

You have to look closely to find me sitting in the top half of the photo on the right side with my students at the elementary school in El Alto. March 1966

I brought my camera to school one day and asked the teachers to take a photo of me with each class. As I posed with my students, the camera recorded some of them holding up a favorite doll, a pencil, or a map they had drawn. The printed photos were later posted in each classroom to the delight of the children.

On another day, before going to class, I gathered together a bunch of American magazines from the Peace Corps office, such as *Life* and *The Saturday Evening Post,* to carry to El Alto. I planned on asking my students to cut out pictures, paste them on paper, and write the English words below. But when I got to school, something unexpected happened.

As I distributed the magazines, the students behaved like hungry wolves, jostling each other and grabbing at the publications, tearing open the pages, whooping and hollering with excitement at the wealth of photos, pointing at all the colorful pictures, and wildly exclaiming over the variety. Every time they saw a picture of a blonde girl in the magazine, they pointed at it and shouted, "*Señorita* Peggy!"

The abundance of merchandise, scenery, and people inside the pages of the magazines had opened up a new world for my students, and I let them explore it. There would be other days for English lessons.

At the school in El Alto, I posed for a photo with my favorite student (with bandage) who loved talking to me during recess. 1966

CHAPTER FIFTEEN
THE OTHER COPACABANA

For years, I'd heard of Brazil's glamorous, sexy Copacabana Beach in Rio de Janeiro, so I was surprised to learn of a Bolivian Christian pilgrimage site also called Copacabana. Could there be a connection between these two seemingly different places? Yes, but not in the way you'd expect.

Copacabana, Bolivia is a small *altiplano* town on the shores of Lake Titicaca where a Catholic church was built in the early 1600s to honor the Virgin of Copacabana and to house "The Dark Virgin," a statue of the Madonna carved by an Inca craftsman from dark cactus wood. According to legend, in 1576, several Brazilian fishermen were caught in a raging storm on Lake Titicaca. When they prayed for help, the Virgin Mary appeared and led them to safety. In gratitude to the Virgin, the Brazilian city of Rio de Janeiro renamed its beautiful beach Copacabana.

One sunny Saturday morning in March 1966, I joined three female Peace Corps Volunteers, on a trip to the fabled town of Copacabana, 99 miles across the *altiplano* from La Paz. We were warmly dressed in blue jeans and winter coats for the cold *altiplano* weather. Our plans were to see the famous church in Copacabana and the nearby *Isla del Sol* (Island of the Sun), a sacred Inca island which, according to Inca mythology, was the birthplace of the Sun God and the first Incan people.

70

Mickey, the Assistant Peace Corps Director who had met me at the airport when I first arrived, was visiting several Volunteers in *altiplano* villages that day and offered us a ride in his four-wheel-drive vehicle. He planned to drop us off in Copacabana and pick us up later in the day on his return to La Paz.

As we traveled across the *altiplano* to Copacabana, we passed big-wheeled transport trucks heading into La Paz. *Campesinos* were standing in the open bed of the truck and holding onto its slatted wood sides. As I looked at their stoic, weathered faces leaning into the fierce, cold wind, I was secretly grateful to be traveling in the comfort of a private, four-wheel-drive vehicle.

In Copacabana, our first stop was the centuries-old Church of the Virgin of Copacabana to see the famous "Dark Virgin" statue. At four feet tall, the black Madonna sat above the altar in a niche decorated with flowers and white clouds painted on a sky blue background. The ebony-colored statue wore a white veil, a crown, and an ornate pink and gold cape and gown, and I thought it was beautiful.

After leaving the church, we climbed to the top of a nearby hill and walked past seven cathedral-shaped, stone shrines depicting the Seven Sorrows of the Virgin. Later, we cruised in a motorboat across the clear sapphire-blue waters of Lake Titicaca, the second largest lake in South America. The lake touches the shores of both Bolivia and Peru and at 12,500 feet above sea level, it's the highest navigable lake in the world. Our motorboat took us to the *Isla del Sol,* to explore archaeological ruins and terraced hillsides typical of the Incan civilization, and then returned us to Copacabana.

Back in town, we headed for a little marketplace in front of the church where *campesina* women sitting on blankets were selling hats, bags, blankets, and medallions of the Virgin. The Warner Brothers Hollywood studio was filming a documentary that day called *The Highest Land*, and we were thrilled when the director asked us to appear in some scenes. Somehow I, who was the least skilled at negotiating prices, was selected to bargain on film with a *campesina* vendor for several handmade reed baskets and a miniature reed boat which I ended up buying. I did my best as the cameras rolled and hoped my scene would make it into the film.

In addition, the studio photographer took a delightful photo of me standing in front of the church and holding the reed handicrafts which practically jump out of the picture. March 1966.

Warner Brothers sent the photo to my hometown newspaper with the caption: "Peggy Dickenson has been serving in Bolivia for seven months as a Peace Corps teacher in a small community near the capital city of La Paz near the famed shrine of the Virgin of the Lake."

By the end of the afternoon, Mickey returned to Copacabana with several Volunteers and a *campesino* in the Peace Corps vehicle, leaving no room for us. A chill went down my spine when Mickey said we had to return to the city in an open-bed truck instead. I remembered how grimy and bedraggled Peace Corps Volunteers looked after traveling into the city this way and wondered if I would suffer the same fate.

In the town plaza, the heavy, big-wheeled transport truck was being readied for its trip across the *altiplano* as *campesinos* loaded it up with crates of live chickens and bags of potatoes, barley, and alpaca wool. The dozen *campesino* men and women waiting to board were wrapped in hats, heavy coats, shawls, ponchos, and blankets for the cold ride, and I prayed my blue jeans and hooded winter coat would protect me from the harsh elements.

When the passengers started to climb aboard, I couldn't reach the high truck bed, so a couple of *campesinos* lifted me up and suggested I hold onto the wood slats on the side of the truck to steady myself. Two *campesina* women smiled as they plopped down in the middle of the truck bed amid the produce and chickens, and we were on our way.

The noisy, exhaust-spewing truck lumbered out of town onto the dirt road that crossed one of the most extensive areas of high plateau on earth. As expected, the trip was windy, cold, and dusty, but surprisingly, it was also fascinating. From my exposed perch, I had a panoramic view of the snow-covered peaks of the distant mountains and the dry, barren beauty of the *altiplano* as we passed through small, mud-colored villages of adobe brick dwellings huddled together in the chilly wind.

When the sun disappeared and afternoon surrendered into evening, the temperature plunged as it grew dark, and I snuggled deeper into my coat to stay warm and reduce the cold wind on my face. After traveling across the *altiplano* for over two hours, the truck started its descent into the city of La Paz and deposited us on the Prado, the main boulevard. Two *campesinos* lifted me off the truck and onto the ground where I regained my equilibrium after the constant rocking and swaying of the vehicle.

I said goodbye to my Peace Corps friends and walked along the Prado looking for a taxi. But I was assaulted by menacing stares from Bolivian men and shunned by the women who quickly averted their eyes. The atmosphere was unsettling, ominous, and frightening. This was different from the curious looks I usually encountered, but why?

The mystery was solved soon enough when a man with contempt in his eyes sidled up to me and hissed in my ear, "*Mala!*" (Bad Girl!), and I immediately knew what sin I had committed. I was wearing blue jeans. Nice girls never wore slacks or jeans in public, only dresses and skirts. Whenever I'd worn blue jeans before, I'd always traveled in a private vehicle and never walked along the Prado. Chastened but wiser, I quickly hurried home to escape the spotlight and digest another hard lesson learned in this foreign land.

CHAPTER SIXTEEN
GETTING IN OVER MY HEAD

Since my first day in Bolivia, I had noticed the attractive, 12-story, tan-colored building on the Prado which housed the University of San Andrés (pictured here). It was the tallest structure in the city. However, as I approached it that March night, I was mystified to see its façade covered  with pockmarks which, upon closer inspection, were actually bullet holes. Apparently, San Andrés had seen plenty of political activity.

Nevertheless, I was optimistic as I walked up to the university to teach Gregg shorthand three nights a week and office procedures two nights a week. My lectures for the latter class were to be completely in Spanish, an ambitious undertaking for someone with my limited fluency, but I thought I could do it.

San Andrés was very different from the University of Túpak Katari where I had taught English the previous year. Túpac Katari, a disorganized institution in a run-down building with low-income students, still hadn't reopened. Therefore, I moved on to teach at San Andrés, an established institution in a modern building with students from relatively privileged backgrounds and staffed with experienced professors and administrators.

There had already been several student demonstrations at San Andrés since the recent election of the new student body president, and there was talk he would show his strength by launching a revolution against the President of the country. The students were a strong force and often on strike. A 1964 curfew decreed that after 11pm, groups of three or more on the street could be arrested, and Bolivia was still in a state of siege.

But I wasn't thinking of politics that night. I had a Gregg shorthand class to teach. I stepped into the brightly lit lobby. Its polished floor was crowded with students, and I pushed my way to my classroom in a large, mostly empty lecture hall with stadium seating and a blackboard. Twenty students, all young women scattered in the first few rows, smiled and warmly greeted me as I went around the room speaking with them to determine their English fluency. They worked as secretaries and wanted to learn Gregg shorthand to take dictation in English.

Shorthand is a system of hand-written outlines (circles, curves, straight lines, and dots) which represent the sound, rather than the spelling, of a word. Secretaries in those days were required to be skilled stenographers, and I had been writing Gregg shorthand for over six years since 1960 when I learned it in college. It was second nature to me now.

I introduced shorthand outlines and combinations by writing them on the blackboard. As the students learned them, they practiced taking dictation and transcribing the shorthand back into English. They were enthusiastic, hard-working, and well disciplined and became my friends.

A student named Maria Eugenia (pictured here) gave me a beautiful, small *aguayo*, a red-blue-and-green striped woolen cloth with the words *Recuerdo de Amor* (Souvenir of Love) woven into the material, and I still treasure it.

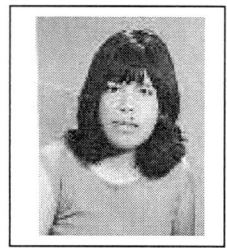

The night before my first office procedures class, I worked late preparing my lecture in Spanish on Carolyn's electric typewriter at the office. It was taking longer than expected, but I was finally ready. However, as I walked into the large lecture hall, I was stunned to see 70 adults of all ages, male and female, staring down at me from the stadium seating.

I introduced myself and launched into my lecture but felt like a fraud. I struggled with my notes, reading my lecture aloud like a robot, and didn't have the fluency for a comfortable give-and-take with the students. Although polite, the students' restlessness and eye contact with each other told me the charade was on borrowed time. In the next three classes, the number of students decreased until a dozen diehards remained. I felt guilty. They weren't getting their money's worth, and I was in way over my head.

To add to the stress, the restrooms at the university were often locked. This was a desperate situation for me on the days I taught at the elementary school in El Alto. On those evenings when I arrived at the university with a full bladder, I had to hunt down a janitor to open the restroom for me, only to find several toilets had overflowed with sewage. I had no choice but to step carefully, hold my nose, and use the facilities anyway.

One Sunday evening, my boyfriend Doug stopped by the Peace Corps office as I was preparing a lecture. He shook some sense into me by decrying, "Why are you killing yourself?" His strong words made me realize I didn't have to take on so many projects to be an effective Peace Corps Volunteer. But how was I going to get out of the office procedures class?

That dilemma was resolved the following week when a San Andrés administrator asked to see me in his office. He thanked me for my efforts and suggested we cancel the office procedures class but continue with the shorthand class. I was greatly relieved. For the next six months, I continued teaching shorthand at San Andrés, but toward the end of that time, something prophetic happened that foretold my future.

One evening, as the bell rang at the end of class, I tried to pull open the classroom door to leave, but it was stuck. I could hear people in the hallway, so I pounded on the door and yelled, "*Abra la puerta, por favor. Está cerrada, y no puedo abrirla.*" (Open the door, please. It's closed, and I can't open it.) Almost immediately, the door was pushed in by a slim, handsome, young Bolivian man with light brown eyes and light brown hair. Our eyes locked for a moment, and as I smiled and thanked him, he smiled back at me. It was fate. Neither of us knew it at the time, but we would meet again the following year in Santa Cruz and fall madly in love.

CHAPTER SEVENTEEN
A REVEALING DAY ON IPANEMA BEACH

Tall and tan and young and lovely
The girl from Ipanema goes walking
And when she passes,
each one she passes, goes - ah.

Music by Antonio Carlos Jobim
English lyrics by Norman Gimbel

The *bossa nova* song, *The Girl from Ipanema*, was a worldwide hit in the 1960s. The words conjured up images of sun-drenched Rio de Janeiro, and whenever I heard Astrud Gilberto's interpretation of the popular tune on the radio, I sang along with her. I had always dreamt of going to Brazil, and now Mary and I were flying there on vacation. It was May 1966.

Our first stop was beautiful Sao Paulo, Brazil's vibrant center of commerce and finance. It reminded me of New York City with its skyscrapers and stylishly-dressed men and women, quite a change from provincial La Paz.

While exploring the energetic city of high-rise office buildings, upscale stores, palm trees and parks, we quickly realized Brazilians didn't understand Spanish. The official language of Brazil is Portuguese, but the only word we knew was *"obrigada"* (thank you), so communication was limited.

After two days in Sao Paulo, we traveled by bus to Rio de Janeiro and checked into the Hotel Riviera, a small, eight-story hotel at the end of Copacabana Beach. Our room had a city view, but we were too excited to sleep that first night, so we ran down the hall to a window with an ocean view and watched the moonlit waves roll onto the sand.

In the morning, we strolled along the Copacabana promenade on its black-and-white mosaic sidewalk decorated in a geometric wave pattern. Across from the beautiful beach stretched a row of beige and cream-colored hotels, restaurants, bars, nightclubs, and residential buildings, from which oozed the syncopated rhythms and sensuous melodies of *bossa nova*, a fusion of jazz and samba.

Brazilians' beautiful faces reflected their European and African heritage, but men followed us everywhere, and the city felt dangerous. After I was pinched on the butt while waiting to cross the street, we decided to tour Rio in the safety of a guide.

Cable cars carried Mary (left) and me (right) to the top of Sugarloaf Mountain on a cloudy day where cyclone-like winds greeted us as we drank in the 360-degree views. Later, a railway car  transported us up Corcovado Mountain where we climbed 200 steps to reach the beautiful, huge Christ the Redeemer Statue which looks down on the city.

The next day, we checked out the world-famous headquarters of Stern Jewelers on a fashionable street in the Ipanema section of Rio. The elegant store specialized in precious and semi-precious stones, but the most I could afford was a simple pearl ring. Afterwards, we stopped in a little shop that featured gingham-checked, bikini bathing suits at a reduced price. Mary bought a blue one and I bought a pink one, and we decided to christen them at Ipanema Beach a few blocks away.

Tourists flocked to Copacabana Beach which boasted a handsome mountain range behind elegant buildings that curved along a beautiful sunlit beach. But the locals preferred Ipanema Beach because it was less crowded. Although it didn't have the glamour of Copacabana, it had the hit song *The Girl from Ipanema,* and that's why we were there.

Mary and I swam in the warm, blue-green waters of Ipanema, but as we were walking out of the surf, it happened. Mary was slightly ahead of me when she turned around to say something, but instead her eyes widened and she yelled, "Get back in the water," as she sprinted past me into the waves. "Why?" I asked. "Our bathing suits are transparent," she screamed. When I looked down, I was horrified to see she was right and quickly jumped back in, too.

How could we not have noticed our bathing suits were unlined? And how were we going to get to our towels without exposing ourselves? Luckily Ipanema wasn't crowded that weekday, so we made a run for it, threw on our beach cover-ups, and headed back to the hotel laughing all the way.

The next day, we lunched with two young women I trained with who were stationed in Rio. Sally, a tall, regal blonde, and Rosemary, a cute, petite brunette worked in the Peace Corps office and taught English. We had all come so far since our training days and entertained each other with stories of our adventures.

Rosemary invited us to a party that evening hosted by a friend of hers at his apartment. At the party, Peace Corps Volunteers and Brazilians mingled together, but one young American man with thick prescription eyeglasses and a toothy smile caught my eye. I knew him from somewhere. He and Rosemary were sitting on a couch, wrapped up in conversation with eyes only for each other. When I told him he looked familiar and asked if I, too, looked familiar, he brushed me off with barely a glance and a brisk "No" and turned his attention back to Rosemary.

But I persisted. Where had he worked? Where had he gone to college? Where had he grown up? Where had he gone to high school? Bingo! His name was Chris, and he had been in my high school class, but only in his senior year. He didn't remember me or anyone else, he said, because it hadn't been a happy year for him. But he looked happy now, and so did Rosemary.

The next day, Mary and I said goodbye to magical Rio and flew to Montevideo, Uruguay. Ah, we were back in a Spanish-speaking country and could easily communicate again.

I called a Peace Corps friend named Christine, a pretty, petite blonde who had trained with me at the

University of Arizona. Christine was stationed in the Montevideo Peace Corps office and took time off to tour the city with us and two of her Peace Corps friends, Gene and Tim, both of whom were obviously in love with her.

Cosmopolitan Montevideo is a seaside port city on the north shore of the Rio de la Plata which separates Uruguay from Argentina. The weather was cold that day, so we bundled up in coats, a big change from wearing bikinis in tropical Rio.

Among the sights in this European-style city were the port market and historic forts, but the highlight was a trip across the bright blue waters of the Bay of Montevideo to the *Cerro de Montevideo* (Montevideo Hill) for an overall view of the city. That evening, Mary and I said goodbye to our friends and rode a ferry across the Rio de la Plata to Buenos Aires, Argentina where we checked into a downtown hotel.

A privately-guided tour by car the next day introduced us to the elegant city of Buenos Aires, known as the Paris of South America, with its colonial architecture, wide boulevards, plazas, theatres, and tango schools. The people were sophisticated and fashionably dressed, and included a surprising number of blond men and women of English and German heritage.

Our introduction to this beautiful country included an Argentine cowboy *gaucho fiesta* at a cattle ranch outside of Buenos Aires. Five handsome young men dressed in loose *gaucho* pants, neck scarves, woolen ponchos, and knee-high leather boots performed an energetic *gaucho* tap dance, followed by the *asado*, a traditional open-fire barbeque of Argentine beef.

Since the government of Argentina had never requested Peace Corps Volunteers, none of my friends from training were there. But Mary was in touch with a Marine guard named Jim whom I remembered seeing at the American Embassy in La Paz. Jim was a handsome, blond young man stationed in Buenos Aires, and Mary gave him a call.

That evening, Jim brought along a Marine buddy named Mike, a medium-tall, dark-haired, stocky young man, and we all went dancing at the Mau Mau Discotheque, a beautiful, modern cavern of red and yellow flashing lights that throbbed to the beat of loud recorded music played by DJs. This was the "in" place to be, and we danced on the polished disco floor to Latin, Brazilian, American, and British music.

In this slightly damaged Polaroid photo, Mary (left) and I (far right) pose with our two Marine guards at the Mau Mau Discotheque in Buenos Aires, Argentina. May 1966.

But like Cinderella, our evening came to an end at midnight. Mary and I had reservations on a night flight to La Paz, so Jim and Mike took us to the airport to see us off, but an airline official told us the landing lights at the La Paz airport had been stolen. When he said our departure from Buenos Aires had to be delayed until there was enough daylight in La Paz for us to land, we laughed and shook our heads in disbelief and settled in for a long night.

Due to the late hour, we told the guys to go home, but our gallant Marine guards insisted on staying with us. The night wore on, and our bright-eyed enthusiasm gave in to stifled yawns and half-closed eyes as we nodded off in the airport lounge until it was time to say goodbye.

Finally, in the wee hours of the morning when it was still dark outside, we hugged our dates goodbye, boarded our flight to Bolivia, and several hours later safely touched down at the La Paz airport in the early light of dawn. In spite of the airport snafu at the end of our whirlwind vacation, it was good to be home again.

CHAPTER EIGHTEEN
A DERBY FOR RIP KIRBY

In August 1966 after almost a year in Bolivia, I was still working in the Peace Corps office and teaching English in El Alto and shorthand at the University of San Andrés. But my love life had changed.

Doug and I had broken up. I was tired of going to Calacoto with him every weekend, and he didn't like

 going to parties with me. Instead, I found romance with a Peace Corps Volunteer from Chicago named Kevin, a young man of Irish descent and wavy red hair (pictured here) who was a professional bricklayer and a talented writer.

Around this time, my father, Fred Dickenson, visited me in La Paz after completing research in Chile on assignment for the *Reader's Digest*. I was looking forward to showing him how rich my new life in Bolivia was, especially since he had initially disapproved of my overseas adventure.

Dad was a newspaper reporter in New York City and wrote the *Rip Kirby* detective comic strip which was owned by King Features Syndicate and drawn by John Prentice. With the exception of my dad's silver hair, he actually looked a lot like the handsome, bespectacled, dark-haired hero of the strip which appeared in more than 400 newspapers all over the world, including Bolivia's *Última Hora*.

When Dad arrived in La Paz, King Features saw an opportunity to promote *Rip Kirby* and hired two affable public relations agents from the Hamilton Wright Organization, an American firm with offices worldwide. A tall, 35-year-old American named Jim and an aristocratic, older Bolivian named George treated my father like a celebrity as they squired him around town.

When I joined them, they invited me to the premiere later that month of a travelogue documentary called *The Highest Land* filmed by Warner Brothers and produced by the Hamilton Wright Organization for the Bolivian government. The film was to be shown in cinemas around the world as a way to promote Bolivia.

Jim and George didn't realize I had been filmed for that movie when I bargained with a *campesina* vendor in front of the Church of the Virgin of Copacabana at Lake Titicaca. But as I described my scene, they exchanged awkward glances and confessed it had been cut, which left me so miffed that I foolishly skipped the screening later that month.

During my father's few days in Bolivia, he stayed at the Hotel Crillon, the best hotel on the Prado. I met him there one morning for more sightseeing, and when I showed him the Peace Corps office and my house, he nodded his approval. Later, while strolling along the Prado, our heads turned in the direction of a passing taxi when a passenger called out my name. The taxi screeched to a halt, and Raul, a short, slim,

24-year-old Bolivian man, and Carlos, his cousin of the same age, ran over to us.

Raul and I had met the previous summer at the University of Arizona where he had studied English to become a tour guide and I had trained for the Peace Corps. Now here we were in Raul's home town of La Paz, far removed from all the stress and hard work of that summer and enjoying the rewards of our efforts. We posed for a photo to commemorate our chance encounter and agreed to meet again.

L-R: Raul, me, my father, and Raul's cousin on the Prado, 1966.

That afternoon, Jim and George arranged for my father to be interviewed by the *Última Hora* newspaper. The flattering article referred to my father as the well-known writer of the famous comic strip *Rip Kirby* whose adventures had delighted millions of readers around the world. Fred Dickenson, it continued, was in Bolivia for a brief visit and promised a future *Rip Kirby* adventure would take place there.

The article also noted Fred Dickenson was in La Paz to see his daughter, a Peace Corps Volunteer teaching at the University of San Andrés. The newspaper photographer caught us by surprise when he placed on my head a derby (or bowler) hat traditionally worn by indigenous females, an unlikely headpiece for a foreigner.

"ULTIMA HORA" La Paz Miércoles 10 de Agosto de 1966

Está en La Paz el autor de la famosa historieta "Rip Kirby" que publican 463 diarios del mundo

Escribirá una aventura de este imaginario personaje en escenarios como Tiahuanacu, Lago Titicaca, La Paz y Yungas.-

Viva sorpresa causó ayer al personal de este diario la noticia de saber que se encuentra en esta ciudad el conocido escritor norteamericano, Fred Dickenson, autor de la famosa historieta "Rip Kirby" que publican alrededor de 463 diarios de todo el mundo.

ULTIMA HORA se sirve de esta historieta desde la creación del célebre personaje, que es distribuida en todo el mundo por la King Features Syndicate, Inc., ofreciendo así permanentemente a su público lector la popular historieta de un célebre personaje imaginario que deleita con sus aventuras a millones de personas en el mundo.

PROPOSITOS DE LA VISITA

El creador del personaje, llegó a Bolivia a invitación de la firma americana encargada de las relaciones públicas de nues-

El señor Fred Dickenson, escritor americano y autor literario de la historieta "Rip Kirby", que se encuentra en La Paz, posa con su hija Peggy que luce el clásico "bombín" de la cholita paceña.

> The headline reads: The author of the famous comic strip "Rip Kirby," which 463 world daily newspapers publish, is in La Paz
>
> The caption reads: Mr. Fred Dickenson, American writer and literary author of the comic strip "Rip Kirby," who is in La Paz, poses with his daughter Peggy who shows off the classic bowler hat of the La Paz indigenous woman.

We got a lot of mileage out of that photo which also appeared in our hometown newspaper with the caption "Rip Kirby and a Derby," noting that Fred Dickenson, the writer of the comic strip, was in Bolivia visiting his daughter whose hat was the typical headgear of the Bolivian Andes.

The following day, Jim and George accompanied us on a day trip to the town of Coroico in the semi-tropical Yungas, 6,000 feet lower than La Paz along 43 miles of what is known as "the most dangerous road in the world." The locals call it "*el camino del muerte*" (the death road) and pray before traveling on it. More fatal car and truck accidents occur along this road than anywhere in the world.

The single-lane dirt road meant for two-way traffic cuts into the steep wall of the mountain and has sheer cliffs that descend thousands of feet to the valley below. Landslides, falling rocks, and waterfalls add to the constant danger. During the bumpy ride, my dad sat on a pillow for extra cushioning, but his slim frame took a beating, and he shot me a sideways glance as our four-wheel-drive vehicle lurched up and down and from side to side. It was a hair-raising trip during which I said a few prayers myself.

Every time we crept up to a blind hairpin curve, our driver honked his horn to warn those coming from the other direction, and they did the same. It was especially dangerous when we encountered big-wheeled, open-bed trucks on their way to the La Paz market loaded with *campesino* passengers, tropical fruit, coffee, and coca leaves. The large trucks stretched across the entire width of the road within inches of the rocky ledge, so we always backed up to an outcropping and allowed them to pass first.

Amid the cacophony of car and truck horns echoing throughout the valley, we saw a *campesina* woman in her traditional derby hat sitting on the mountainside calmly chewing dried coca leaves like a cow chewing its cud. Coca leaves are cultivated in the Yungas and sold in the La Paz marketplace. In its raw state, the coca leaf produces a pleasurable numbness, and the indigenous people have chewed it for centuries as a way to cope with cold temperatures, high altitude, hunger, thirst, pain, and fatigue.

Countless wooden and metal crosses planted in the rocky soil honored those who had lost their lives in car accidents. But it gave us pause to read the inscription on a carved, 4x6-foot stone monument in memory of several politicians who had been murdered when they were thrown over the cliff in the 1940s.

The sky was overcast and gray during most of the trip, but as we descended into the Yungas, the bright sun broke through, highlighting breathtaking landscape views of the majestic emerald-green mountains amid lush valleys of waving palm trees and garlands of red, pink, and orange flowers. The soft, warm, tropical breezes and oxygen-rich air revived our spirits after the harshness of Bolivia's cold highlands.

Following a leisurely lunch, we relaxed that afternoon amid banana trees and orange groves at the picturesque Hotel Prefectoral with its red tile roof, white-washed stucco walls, and round archways until it was time to bid farewell and travel back to chilly La

Paz where we arrived in the late afternoon, tired and a bit sore but thankful for a safe trip.

My father flew home the next day and in December of that year wrote a storyline for the comic strip in which Rip Kirby and his trusty butler Desmond arrived in La Paz to search for a woman named Lyra Lynn who had information about a murder. While there, they coped with the high altitude, sat at an outdoor café, and enjoyed the festivities of *Carnaval*. Even Lyra Lynn joined the festival parade when a dancer wearing a bear costume picked her out of the crowd. This was a nod to my *Carnaval* experience in Oruro where the same thing had happened to me. The *Rip Kirby* readers in Bolivia must have been pleased, and I was, too.

In this English language version of the *Rip Kirby* comic strip, the storyline takes place in La Paz, Bolivia. It was later translated into Spanish for the Latin American newspapers.

Panel 1: Lyra Lynn thinks: I'll stay here in La Paz, forget I ever knew Jack Page, and in time they'll all forget me.
Panel 2: BUT JUST OUTSIDE…Desmond says: I'll be glad to rest, sir. I really do feel exertion at this high altitude. Rip says: All right, Desmond. Take it easy here and keep an eye open for Lyra Lynn.
Panel 3: Rip says: I'm going to look further about the city. If you see her, try to get a line on where she's staying.

CHAPTER NINETEEN
A SPECIAL VISIT TO EL ALTO

In October 1966, two months after my father left La Paz, my mother visited me. Before arriving in Bolivia, she toured Rio de Janeiro and Buenos Aires with local guides. But it had been a lonely trip, and she looked tired when I met her at the airport. She was glad to finally be with me. We were best friends.

My mother had, in her youth, been a brunette beauty. In 1936, she served as one of the first United Airlines stewardesses, a glamorous career in those early days of flying, and she was often photographed for the newspapers. One reporter who interviewed her was my father, and they married the following year. But stewardesses had to be unmarried, so Mom hung up her uniform and pursued other interests.

My parents lived in New York City, and Mom's love of theater led to work as a model and actress in summer stock and off-Broadway. She was even offered a Hollywood screen test, but my parents decided it was time to start a family instead. I was the first-born, followed 22 months later by my twin sisters, Elizabeth and Virginia, and my mother became a full-time homemaker.

While visiting me in La Paz, Mom stayed at the Copacabama Hotel, one of the best hotels on the Prado. Her fourth-floor window afforded a bird's-eye view of the activities along the main boulevard and the colorful red-and-blue mosaic designs on the beautifully landscaped sidewalk in the middle of the Prado. An early riser, she loved watching the indigenous women in their derby hats and full skirts sweep the empty sidewalks every morning with bunches of straw banded together. And later in the day, she got a kick out of the young men who hung onto the outside of small, overcrowded buses.

My mother I pose on the sidewalk in the middle of the Prado.

Behind us on the left is a corner of the Copacabana Hotel where Mom stayed.

After Sunday morning Mass, Mary, Mom and I joined the *paseo*, a promenade held at midday every Sunday after the sun warmed up the cold mountain air. Young men in suits and ties walked clockwise around the center sidewalk of the Prado, and young women in dresses walked counter-clockwise in order to smile at a possible suitor, all under the watchful eyes of the elders who sat on park benches.

The next day, among our sightseeing plans, was a trip to the elementary school in El Alto. We splurged on a taxi which I hailed on The Prado, and since we were going out of the city, I negotiated a price with the driver.

My students knew we'd be coming, but when we arrived, they went wild with excitement, thrilled that someone from America had come to see them. In each class, the students greeted my mother in English, as we had practiced, and smiled and giggled when she greeted them back. But eventually our visit caused so much pandemonium that the children had to be excused for recess.

My mother took this picture during recess as the children ran toward the camera. The Church of the Nazarene is behind them.

When we said goodbye, a flood of students followed us to our waiting taxi and surrounded it, but the driver complained about the commotion, and I was afraid he was going to run over a child. Finally, the students made an opening for us, and we were able to slowly pull away. Looking back through the rear window of the taxi, I watched as my students ran behind us, laughing, waving, and yelling goodbye until the taxi picked up speed and left them in the dust. My mother whispered to me it was the best day of her trip.

Every evening, we ate at the best restaurants, but Mom was suffering the headaches and nausea of altitude sickness and couldn't eat. I suggested we take a taxi to the stadium where indigenous women in derby hats barbecued skewers of meat, potatoes, and vegetables at food stalls outside the arena. Mom loved the freedom of walking around and breathing the cold night air and was able to eat some food.

As we stood in the sparsely crowded, dimly lit area around the arena and slid the hot, juicy food off the skewers with our teeth, three adorable indigenous children appeared, looking up at us with their big brown eyes and begging for money. They melted my mother's heart, and she reached for her purse, but Mary and I warned her not to do so and to beware of pickpockets. Nevertheless, Mom doled out some coins to the children, and as if on signal, twenty screaming children came out of the shadows, surrounding us in a mad rush, pushing and grabbing. We quickly hailed a taxi to escape the chaos, while Mom, sheepish and contrite, conceded we had been right.

The following day, Raul, my Bolivian tour guide friend, escorted my mother and me to the *altiplano* to see the pre-Incan ruins of an ancient empire called Tiahuanaco. The site was in a poor state of preservation due to ancient floods and earthquakes plus centuries of looting, but it was finally being restored. The best preserved structure was the Gateway to the Sun, a portal carved from a single block of granite, but much was left to do to make this a must-see for tourists.

The next day, however, we were on our way to one of the most famous and beautifully restored archeological sites in the world – Peru's Machu Picchu. But the trip would sorely test our endurance.

CHAPTER TWENTY
MAGICAL MACHU PICCHU

Our trip to Machu Picchu started off well with an afternoon ride in a sparsely filled railroad car across the *altiplano* to the small Bolivian port of Guaqui on Lake Titicaca.

From there, we transferred to a handsome, 165-foot iron steamboat for a leisurely overnight cruise across Lake Titicaca's sapphire blue waters to Puno, Peru. Our small but comfortable first-class private cabin of polished wood and brass accents, two bunk beds with crisp white sheets, a porcelain sink, and a view of the lake through a brass porthole offered a taste of elegance I hadn't experienced in a while.

In the late afternoon light, we cruised past Aymara Indian boatmen wearing *llama* wool ponchos and colorful knit wool Andean hats with earflaps as they sat in their reed-bundled, crescent-shaped boats, a traditional form of transportation for centuries. And in our cozy shipboard dining room, we joined a dozen friendly travelers from all over the world at a large wooden table. Conversations in French, German, Spanish, and English swirled around us as we dined on a delicious dinner served by waiters. Before going to bed, Mom and I walked around the deck under a full moon as we listened to the gentle waves lap against the hull. At Puno the next morning, scrambled eggs, fruit, croissants, coffee and tea, were served, a hearty breakfast that would prove to be our last meal for more than 24 hours.

We transferred to a train crowded with locals and a few tourists and settled into our comfortable seats for the ten-hour ride to Cuzco. The train eased out of the station, skirted along the lake, and passed through prairie flatlands before climbing into the Andean mountains. At one stop, two men ran through the car carrying a freshly-killed animal dripping with blood and set it on the floor next to our seat. Thankfully, they got off at the next station with their prize but left behind a small puddle of blood.

At each dusty stop, local indigenous women and children surged toward the train windows, holding up bread, fruit, vegetables, and textiles for sale. But when they spotted my mother and me, they pushed and jostled each other to stand under our window and scream at us while plying their wares. We quickly learned to scrunch down in our seats and turn our faces away from the window when the train stopped. Due to the unsanitary conditions, it was too risky to eat this food, so we decided to wait until Cuzco.

Toward evening, as we traveled through the mountains, threatening clouds darkened the sky and rain poured down. Everyone was dozing when the train suddenly lurched to a stop. A massive rockslide had fallen on the tracks, and when I looked out the window, a raging river roared below us and the train hovered precariously close to the edge. In the dark of night after an endless wait, we abandoned our train, climbed over the rockslide, and boarded a train on the other side that carried us to Cuzco. But it was midnight when we finally arrived in the historic capital of the Incan empire, exhausted, hungry, and too late for dinner.

To make matters worse, the desk clerk at our hotel had no record of our reservation. He told us to check with the hotel in the next block, so Mom and I trudged up a steep hill by the light of the moon and a dim street lamp on a deserted, wet cobblestone street, carrying our luggage at 11,000 feet above sea level. But that hotel had no vacancies, either. "Go back to the first hotel and demand a room," my mother said, so we did and this time, the desk clerk gave us a room. I requested an early morning call so we could eat breakfast before leaving for Machu Picchu, and we collapsed into bed.

The next morning, I woke with a start and the sinking feeling that it was late. There had been no wakeup call. When I looked at the clock, we had 15 minutes before our tour left, just enough time to brush our teeth and throw on some clothes, but too late for breakfast. We rushed to join a group of international tourists who were boarding a bus to the train station for the three-and-a-half hour trip to Machu Picchu.

As our train traveled alongside the roaring Urubamba River into the Sacred Valley of tall, green, jagged mountains blanketed by fog and light rain, we shared our survival story with our traveling companions who marveled that adrenalin and determination alone had kept us going. When the train stopped at the base of a mountain, we boarded a bus for a stomach-churning, 25-minute ride along a narrow dirt road that crisscrossed back and forth across the steep mountain like an amusement park ride. We laughed when the middle-aged American woman in front of us murmured to her husband, "There's a certain travel agent back home whose neck I'm going to throttle."

And then we were there – at magical, mystical Machu Picchu, the Lost City of the Incas. A hush fell over us as we gazed at the spiritual site which exuded a powerful presence. The rain stopped, the fog lifted, and the sun came out, highlighting the classical Inca architecture of the buildings spread throughout on a carpet of grass with a backdrop of lush, green, mountains kissed by the clouds. The scene at 8,000 feet above sea level was breathtaking.

Before exploring the site, our group sat together for lunch at a large table in the hotel restaurant on the edge of the ruins. Mom and I gobbled down more than our fair share of bread, followed by hot soup and a hearty meal. We had never been so hungry.

Then the tour guide, a short, middle-aged Peruvian man who spoke Spanish and English, led our multi-lingual group up and down the stone steps to the temples, residences, sanctuaries, storage buildings, and water fountains where white *llamas* freely roamed. At each stop, he spoke in Spanish for 5-10 minutes and in English for only about two minutes, so I filled Mom in on some of the information he failed to translate, while other English speakers grumbled at the discrepancy.

I posed among the Incan ruins at Machu Picchu, October 1966.

The guide explained that the Incas built Machu Picchu in 1452, perhaps as a sacred religious site or a royal residence, but abandoned it a century later. The Spanish conquistadors, who destroyed everything in their path, never discovered the location, and it was unknown to the outside world, so Machu Picchu was a relatively intact cultural site when the American historian, Hiram Bingham, discovered it in 1911.

The buildings were constructed of enormous, polished blocks of stone notched and fitted together so perfectly without mortar that not even a blade of grass can fit between them. How the Incas were able to move huge blocks of stone up the mountain, place them on top of each other, and cut them to fit is one of the many mysteries of Machu Picchu. For a long time, we just sat and contemplated the beauty and peacefulness of this enchanted place, but soon it was time to leave, and in the late afternoon, we boarded a train that carried us back to Cuzco.

The next day, I said goodbye to my mother who flew to Lima and New York while I returned to La Paz by train and steamboat, all without incident. Of all our travel experiences and in spite of everything that went wrong on this trip, we agreed that Machu Picchu was the best.

CHAPTER TWENTY-ONE
TRANSFER TO SANTA CRUZ

Early one October morning, my boss Al Purcell called me into his office and in his reserved manner, calmly dropped a bombshell. He was transferring me to the Santa Cruz office. Janice, the Volunteer secretary in that semi-tropical outpost, was completing her two years of service; and Maryann, my training buddy, who had been working with Janice to take her place, was transferring to the Guatemala Peace Corps office. She had been unhappy in Santa Cruz and wanted out. Although I was apprehensive about what lay in store, I was ready for a new adventure.

I said goodbye to my students at the elementary school in El Alto and the University of San Andrés, made my airline reservations, and packed my bags. My roommate Mary was going to stay in the house we had shared and keep in touch via shortwave radio. As for my redheaded boyfriend, Kevin, we spent the evening together before my departure, and he offered to accompany me to the airport, but it was late by the time I got home.

The next morning dawned bright and sunny as I waited with my luggage for Kevin to come by in a taxi. I appreciated his offering to do so, because I lived on a quiet side street where vacant taxis never cruised by. However, he was late. In despair, I hid my luggage behind a wall and went inside the main house to call him. But my heart sank when I woke him up, and as he fumbled for the phone, he croaked, "I'm not gonna make it." I hung up, my heart beating wildly, ran down the hill to a busy street, quickly hailed a taxi, rode back up the hill to pick up my luggage, and after an endless ride to the El Alto airport, arrived just in time for my flight to Santa Cruz on a LAB Airline DC-3.

The City of Santa Cruz is located in the Department of Santa Cruz, a huge region stretching across the eastern part of Bolivia to the borders of Brazil and Paraguay.

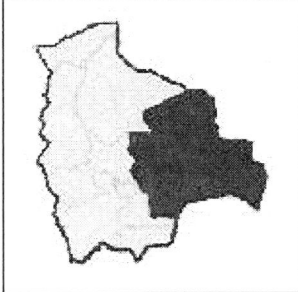

In this map of Bolivia, the Department of Santa Cruz is highlighted in black. The city of Santa Cruz is located in the western half of the Department.

Clear blue skies and a green, flat, tree-filled landscape greeted me as we flew into El Trompillo, the small Santa Cruz airport. As I stepped off the airplane into the hot, humid air and walked across the dusty tarmac to the airline terminal building, my heart was touched by an old man with a clubfoot who was wearing a wide-brimmed straw hat and waiting for customers by his shoeshine stand.

Several taxis, all Willys Jeeps with canvas tops, plastic windows, and no doors, were lined up. I climbed into one after piling my luggage into the back seat, and we took off for the short ride into the city. Slowly creeping along the unpaved, uneven roads, the jeep churned up clouds of dust, occasionally rocking back and forth in and out of deep ruts in the road while I held onto the seat frame to keep from falling out. There were no traffic lights and little traffic.

Santa Cruz was the third largest city in Bolivia, but it looked like a wild-West frontier town. None of the streets were paved, the dusty sidewalks were raised above the ground, horses were tied to hitching posts, and ox-drawn carts were a familiar sight. It was like stepping back in time.

As the taxi entered the heart of the city, we circled around the central plaza, the middle of which boasted a lush green park of palm fronds and tall, leafy trees which provided a cooling canopy of shade. Also in abundance were colorful flowers, white wood-slat park benches, tropical birds, and tree-dwelling *perezosos* (which means lazy), the slow-moving, gray-colored sloths that appear to be smiling and hang upside down.

Around the perimeter of the central plaza were two outdoor cafes, a large cathedral with twin bell towers called the Basilica de San Lorenzo; and white, Spanish colonial, two-and-three-story white stucco and brick buildings with red terra-cotta tiled roofs supported by large, round, white columns connected by arches which formed porticos around the plaza.

The taxi turned down a side street and stopped in front of the *Residencial Bolivar*. This was to be my temporary home and also housed other Peace Corps Volunteers who came into the city to pick up supplies or meet with officials. The entryway of the 18th Century Spanish colonial house led to an inner courtyard with brick tile, orchids, palm trees, ferns, banana trees, red and orange flowers, hammocks, and a tame, colorful toucan bird with a large orange bill.

Each room opened onto the courtyard, and I settled into a small, stuffy one just big enough for a bed and my luggage. That night, as I was dozing off, a large bug crawled across my arm, sending me flying to the ceiling. Now I understood why mosquito netting over the bed was recommended, as well as shaking out one's shoes before putting them on.

The next morning, I was awakened by laughter coming through the open window. A handsome, blond Peace Corps Volunteer named Gus was grinning rakishly and sitting on a horse he had ridden from his *campo* village to Santa Cruz and into the courtyard, amusing everyone except the owner who told him to get the heck out of there.

After breakfast, I walked several blocks on sand-covered sidewalks to the Peace Corps office located in an earth-colored, two-story storefront building with thin decorative bars on the windows and a blue sign over the front door spelling out *Cuerpo de Paz* (Peace Corps) in red painted letters.

Two street scenes in the city of Santa Cruz, one in dry weather on the left, and one in wet weather on the right.

Janice, the tall, young, brunette Volunteer secretary I was replacing, greeted me in her office to the right of the entryway where I heard static from the shortwave radio sitting on a little table. An oscillating fan on top of a gray metal file cabinet cooled the air, and a black wall telephone, a manual typewriter, chairs, a wooden desk, and a hand-cranked mimeograph machine rounded out the furnishings. A pretty red and green tile floor stretched throughout the building.

Directly across the hall, Janice introduced me to Archie, a slim, good-looking, young Bolivian man who handled financial matters and served as the liaison between Santa Cruz officials and the Peace Corps. A manually-operated adding machine with a handle sat on his desk, and a heavy, gray steel safe with a dial combination lock crouched in a corner of the room. We spoke in Spanish, and Archie showed his good nature and sense of humor by explaining that his real name was Arril, but his American fiancée, Marty, had difficulty pronouncing it, so she gave him the nickname Archie.

Next to Archie's office was that of the Santa Cruz Regional Peace Corps Director, an American named Big Al because of his large size of over six feet tall and a wide girth, who wore a moustache and a friendly smile. Big Al was easy-going and much beloved by the staff and Volunteers.

Mario, a cheerful, slim, Bolivian 18-year-old, ran errands and cleaned the office. He kept the refrigerator in the kitchen stocked with bottles of Pepsi and ice made from boiled and filtered water. Up a flight of stairs, were the library filled with English-language paperbacks for Volunteers to borrow and the office of the Peace Corps doctor, a young bespectacled American named Lee. He looked like a college professor with an unlit tobacco pipe clenched between his teeth, but he had a mischievous grin and showed an inordinate interest in my love life.

Janice trained me for a week and then flew home. My duties were similar to those I had in La Paz, and I quickly settled in. Big Al was often in the *campo* visiting Volunteers in their villages, many of which were Jesuit mission towns from the mid-1700s, such as San Ignacio and San Javier, so Archie and I ran the office. We had an easy rapport and laughed a lot. A man of integrity and generosity, Archie was supportive and kind as I learned the ropes of my new job and living in Santa Cruz. This was a smaller office than the one in La Paz, and I loved it.

I also loved living at the *Residencial Bolivar* and didn't look for permanent lodging for three weeks until Big Al warned me I would have to pay the room charge if I stayed any longer. That was the kick in the pants I needed, and I got busy looking for a new home.

CHAPTER TWENTY-TWO
HOT TEMPERATURES
AND COLD SHOWERS

Archie knew of a room for rent two blocks from the office in the home of *Señora* Virginia on Nuflo de Chavez, a street named for the man who founded Santa Cruz in 1561. The one-story, gray-painted, attached residences on the street presented a uniform look lined up next to each other, and the roofs which extended over the dusty sidewalks to provide shade were supported by simple wooden posts.

The S*eñora*, a cheerful, middle-aged Bolivian woman, warmly greeted me as I followed her through the pretty inner courtyard decorated with potted plants and vines to my room painted a beautiful robin's-egg blue with a large window that opened onto the courtyard and a private bathroom. Breakfast was included, and I immediately felt at home. Since I already had a *pensión* for lunch and dinner at a restaurant in the central plaza, I was all set.

The Peace Corps office gave me a mosquito net that attached to poles at each corner of my bed, and I loved sleeping in the cocoon it formed. As if to prove its usefulness, when I woke up every morning, a bug or two that had expired during the night would be lying upside down on top of the netting.

Señora Virginia lived with her five-year-old grandson, a mischievous little boy named Cirito. He was a sweet child, but he tested my patience when I took a shower. Although the climate was hot and humid, I had to steel myself every morning to stand under the cold water coursing down my back. Cirito, pictured

 here with *Señora* Virginia, liked to peek through my bathroom window and spy on my naked body. But whenever I spotted him, I'd yell, "Cirito!," and the *Señora* would scold him as he ran away.

The *Señora* sold luscious strawberry, vanilla, and chocolate ice cream out of her home to the neighborhood children. The tasty treat made my mouth water, but when she offered me a taste, I had to make an excuse. Peace Corps training taught me to avoid ice cream because it was made from non-pasteurized milk. Nevertheless, in spite of following the rules and rejecting salads, fruit, ice cream, and non-bottled drinks for two years, I still suffered frequent intestinal problems.

Most of the population of Santa Cruz was mestizo and white and included long-established settlers from Southern Spain, indigenous migrants from the highlands, and immigrants from Europe, Japan, Brazil, and Chile. By contrast, the highlands of La Paz and the *altiplano* were dominated by the Aymara and Quechua indigenous people. The culture and geography of the two regions resulted in differences in climate, history, music, food, dress, and life style, and I was lucky to experience both.

Life in Santa Cruz was at a slow and relaxed pace with a two-hour *siesta* during the hottest part of the day when all the stores and offices closed. Every weekday after lunch at my *pension*, I walked home, took a nap, and returned to the office refreshed. But one day as I was walking back to work, I was startled to see a huge, black, hairy tarantula prancing down the middle of the still empty street as though it owned the place, so I gave it a wide berth.

I communicated every day with the La Paz and Cochabamba Peace Corps offices via the shortwave radio in my office (pictured here) and occasionally spoke with Mary, my housemate in La Paz.

Another daily duty was a trip to the post office to pick up Peace Corps mail. As I strolled under the shade of the extended roofs to the central plaza and through the tall archway of the white stucco, colonial -style, two-story *Correo Central* (Central Post Office), jeep taxis passed by, kicking up dust which assaulted my throat, nose, and eyes. But when it rained, it was even worse, turning the streets into rivers of mud.

From the post office, I continued past the colonial buildings housing the private *Club Social*, the *Cine*

Palace (the Movie Palace), the City Hall, and the Gabriel René Moreno University, and crossed the street to the north side of the plaza to the *Banco Central* (Central Bank), an attractive, four-story building set back from the street with steps leading up to a landing and an arched entryway. From there, I could look across the plaza to the sidewalk cafés, the Basilica de San Lorenzo, and other colonial buildings housing shops, offices, and restaurants, including my *pensión.* Everything was located around the central plaza within easy reach of my home and office.

In the evening after the heat cooled down, Santa Cruz came alive, especially in the plaza, the center of city life and the social meeting place for everyone. After work, I often met friends at one of the sidewalk cafés. My favorite was *La Pascana* (an old word meaning a resting place for travelers on a long journey).

A friend named Mario stands on the patio of *La Pascana.* A policeman's traffic stand is in the foreground.

La Pascana was located on a street corner in a one-story, pale pink stucco building with a small patio in front enclosed by a waist-high, wrought-iron fence and gate. Blond-colored wooden tables and chairs filled the patio and the space inside. Ice cream, *salteñas* (a small meat and vegetable pastry), snacks, and bottles of beer, soda, and mineral water were available. I usually ordered a bottle of Pepsi or mineral water but had to skip the ice, another Peace Corps recommendation.

From its prime location near the Basilica de San Lorenzo whose church bells chimed every quarter hour, *La Pascana* offered an always changing view of people walking through the plaza, meeting friends, discussing politics or business with colleagues, sitting on park benches, and relaxing. Everyone passed through the plaza at one time or another and because of the warm climate, men dressed casually in short-sleeved, open collared shirts and women in short-sleeved cotton dresses.

Sunday evenings were special because that was the night of the *paseo* (promenade) when young men and women walked in opposite directions around the park in the center of the plaza, exchanging glances as their elders watched from park benches. The *paseo* was held in La Paz at midday when the sun warmed up the air, but it was held in Santa Cruz in the evening when the air cooled down. A Bolivian friend named Nelva accompanied me on a *paseo* one Sunday evening, and we checked out the attractive, young men in town.

CHAPTER TWENTY-THREE
THE VIRGIN OF COTOCA

In the Peace Corps office, I met Phil, a young, blond Volunteer, who invited me to join a local choral group he directed. One evening, in a small meeting room near the plaza, he introduced me to twenty pretty, dark-haired young women who welcomed me with open arms. The sopranos made room for me as I sat down, and Phil led us in two-part harmony.

Our repertoire included local folk songs in Spanish (*Viva Santa Cruz*), Brazilian folk songs in Portuguese (*Na Bahia Tem* which means *In Bahia Town*), and my favorite, *Piama*, an Amazonian Indian song from the Beni region north of the Department of Santa Cruz. We created beautiful harmonies under Phil's direction.

On Christmas Day, we performed first at the jail, located ironically at the end of *Calle Libertad* (Liberty Street), where young male prisoners looked sad and just stared at us. Then we sang at the San Juan de Dios hospital where most of the patients smiled as we passed their rooms, and finally at the orphanage where excited children ran toward us on the grounds and gathered around to listen. By sharing the holiday spirit and bringing some happiness into their lives, I forgot how much I missed my own family. It was one of my best Christmases.

Phil was engaged to a pretty Japanese woman named María, who had moved with her family to Santa Cruz where there was a large colony of

Japanese immigrants. When Phil and María married at the end of October 1966, all the Peace Corps Volunteers in the area attended the celebration.

Peace Corps Volunteers at Phil and María's wedding in Santa Cruz, October 1966. I'm standing in the front row on the left holding a drink. Behind me and wearing glasses is John. Standing on the far right are (R-L): Gus, Margaret, Rae (behind Margaret), the groom Phil, and his bride María.

I had met many of these Volunteers when they first arrived in La Paz. One was my good friend, Margaret, a dark-haired beauty of Irish heritage who was a registered nurse. She worked with the local hospital and encouraged staff to put screens on the windows and fold sheets of newspaper into wastebaskets so each room had a garbage receptacle. Margaret also coordinated a training program for young women from *campo* villages and taught them how to deliver babies and use sterile technique for injections and cutting the umbilical cord, plus basic nursing skills and nutrition.

Another Peace Corps buddy was John, a tall, energetic, outgoing guy with glasses, whom I dated a couple of times in La Paz before he went to Santa Cruz. John worked in a tuberculosis-control program and also hosted a local radio show on Sunday nights on *Radio Grigota* during which he talked about Peace Corps projects and played music. One evening he featured a young Peace Corps Volunteer, a pretty African-American named Rae, who played the guitar and sang American folk songs in her beautiful mellow voice.

I also sang with Rae and played the guitar one evening in a small auditorium at the Gabriel René Moreno University in a corner of the plaza. Our voices blended well as we sang Santa Cruz folk songs, and the students applauded us warmly. When my officemate, Archie, requested an American song, Rae demurred, saying she wanted to sing only in Spanish, but she changed her mind, and we ended our performance with Bob Dylan's *Blowing in the Wind*.

I didn't realize our little concert had made such an impression until Archie, who grew up in Santa Cruz and went to college in Buenos Aires, told me the students had never seen anything like it before. Santa Cruz had been isolated for centuries until the first rural paved road in the country was built between Cochabamba and Santa Cruz just ten years earlier, and there was still no television in Bolivia. To see two American women, one white and one black, singing Santa Cruz folk songs with North American accents was apparently quite a curiosity.

Another curiosity was the variety of foreigners in Santa Cruz, including Mormon missionaries, young men with crew cuts who traveled in pairs and wore white short-sleeved shirts, narrow black ties, black pants, and black shoes and carried black-bound copies of the Book of Mormon. When I saw them on the street, they nodded in recognition but kept to themselves, totally devoted to the mission of spreading their religion.

I also knew some young Germans serving in the German Peace Corps. One afternoon at *La Pascana*, I spoke with one of them, a very good-looking blond named Miguel. We communicated in Spanish and understood each other in spite of our grammatical errors. But when local *Cruceños* sitting nearby eavesdropped on our conversation, they couldn't help but laugh at our version of Spanish.

In this blurry photo taken in December 1966, Miguel (left) and I joined another German named Luter (right) and his Santa Cruz girlfriend, Nelva, a pretty girl with long dark hair, for a trip to Cotoca.

We rode in a jeep taxi, rocking along the unpaved road, kicking up clouds of dust to a little town 10 miles into the *campo*. In this Catholic country, it was traditional for each town to celebrate the Virgin Mary with a statue named after the town. The church in Copacabana boasted the famous "Black Virgin" statue of the Virgin of Copacabana. And now we were going to Cotoca for the *fiesta* honoring the Virgin of Cotoca.

Hundreds of other people also made the pilgrimage that day, and the town was packed. Everyone wore white, including Miguel, Luter, and Nelva, but I, unaware of this custom, was inappropriately dressed in a blue denim dress with red cord lacing across a V-neckline. Luckily, no one seemed to care.

In Cotoca, we wandered among the local vendors' tables offering food, pottery, souvenirs, miniature shrines of the Virgin, rosaries, and other religious artifacts. And then the main event began at the far end of the unpaved street where several men carrying the statue of the Virgin of Cotoca were enveloped in a cloud of dust as spectators making the sign of the cross surrounded them. The beautiful, four-foot-high statue, clothed in a long white gown with a glistening gold crown and full-length veil of white lace, stood atop a platform supported by wooden beams that rested on the shoulders of the men who slowly made their way through the crowd. Everyone wanted to be close to the Virgin, and the ceremony was a cause for joyous celebration, not in a quiet contemplative way, but in a glorious, exuberant display of love and affection.

The *fiesta* of the Virgin of Cotoca was memorialized in a Santa Cruz folk song called *A Cotoca* (*To Cotoca*) which our choral group sang, and it became one of my favorites.

CHAPTER TWENTY-FOUR
EL CABALLITO NIGHTCLUB

Many evenings, I rode in a taxi with friends to *El Caballito* (The Little Horse), a popular nightclub some distance from the plaza in the outskirts of Santa Cruz. When we saw the white, neon-lit sign of a prancing horse kicking up its heels in front of the club, we knew we were there.

Although the outside wall of the one-story brick building was embedded with broken pieces of glass, the interior was much more inviting. Wooden tables and chairs encircled a generous dance floor, one wall opened up to a patio allowing the night air to cool the club, and a raised stage at the far end hosted bands that performed Latin, Brazilian, British, and American music. It was here I learned to *samba* and dance to lively Brazilian *Carnaval* music, a completely different genre from the haunting Andean *Carnaval* music I had heard the year before in La Paz and Oruro.

One evening at the club, my favorite band, *Los Blackbirds,* was playing and singing Beatles songs. I hadn't seen the four Brazilian musicians since La Paz, and when they waved to me, it was like old times.

With the dawning of 1967, everyone's thoughts turned to *Carnaval* (Carnival), an annual cultural event celebrated throughout Latin America before the Catholic observance of Lent. The year before, I had witnessed the *Carnaval* parade of Devil Dancers and

120

choreographed costumed dancers in Oruro, but *Carnaval* in Santa Cruz would be completely different due to the influence of its neighbor Brazil.

Carnaval festivities in Santa Cruz began in January with *comparsa* parties. (A *comparsa* is a group that wears the same costume.) Archie invited John and me to attend a Hawaiian party at *El Caballito* for the *comparsa* he belonged to called *Los Aribibis,* which means small, red-hot peppers.

I prepared a costume for the party by wrapping green crepe paper around my two-piece bathing suit and adding strips of green crepe paper to simulate a Hawaiian grass skirt. A white carnation behind my ear, a flower lei, and open-toed wedge sandals completed the look. I was proud of my little paper costume and prayed it wouldn't rain.

When I met John before the party, I was surprised at his outfit. He had gone a different route, perhaps inspired by Billis, the male character in the musical *South Pacific* who performs a comedy burlesque as Honey Bun wearing a blond wig, grass skirt, and coconut-shell bra. John's Bolivian landlady had helped him create his costume: a shoulder-length blond wig and a tropical-patterned fabric wrapped around a woman's bra and John's bathing trunks. If there had been an award for most creative, John would have won.

But creativity wasn't on the agenda that night; conformity was. When we entered *El Caballito*, the members of the *comparsa,* thirty young, beautiful men and women of the Santa Cruz aristocracy, were dressed alike in beautiful shirts, sarong wraps, and sleeveless or strapless dresses all made from the same colorful, floral Hawaiian fabric. Our cartoon-like costumes clashed with the classy, elegant look of the *comparsa*. There were some amused glances our way, and I felt a little embarrassed, but no one seemed to care, because anything goes during *Carnaval*.

Some of the members of the *comparsa* party at *El Caballito* in Santa Cruz. John is on the far right, and I am next to him. Archie and his fiancée, Marty, are in the center, partially obscured by hanging paper streamers.
January 1967

El Caballito was beautifully decorated that evening in a Hawaiian theme with woven straw-mats on the floor; tiki torches, lanterns, colorful tropical flowers of hibiscus, orchids, and carnations, bowls of pineapples, grapes, bananas, and papayas, and paintings of green ferns and palm fronds on wood panels.

Tropical fruit drinks and beer were served, and two bands played. A local group played Santa Cruz *taquirari* dance music, and a band from Brazil played Brazilian *Carnaval* music. My favorite Brazilian

Carnaval song was *A Banda* (*The Band* in Portuguese). It always brought everyone onto the dance floor where couples faced each other and raised their index fingers in the air, alternately moving their fingers up and down to the beat and their bodies and feet to the lively rhythm of the music.

At one point during the evening, Mario, a handsome, bearded Brazilian, asked for someone to dance with him, and I couldn't resist volunteering, as pictured here.

The *comparsa* party was just the start of *Carnaval*, and the best part was yet to come, but it would also bring more opportunities for costume gaffes.

CHAPTER TWENTY-FIVE
CARNAVAL IN SANTA CRUZ

After the *comparsa* parties, *Carnaval* officially began in February on the Saturday before Lent which meant the return of water balloons and the anxiety I felt in Oruro when I was soaked to the skin. To avoid being attacked, and since our office was closed for the holiday, I hunkered down in my room all day and ventured out only to my *pensión* for meals.

Before leaving the house, I surveyed outside my front door for water balloons, then scurried like a little mouse down to the corner, looked both ways, scurried down to the next corner, and so on until I reached my *pensión*. I returned home the same way and, with luck, escaped detection.

But a bigger danger lurked beneath the surface. It was the rumored presence of Che Guevara, the Argentine revolutionary who fought with Fidel Castro in Cuba. Che was suspected of trying to foment another revolution, this time in the rural lowlands and mountains of the Department of Santa Cruz. But those concerns were set aside for the moment, because *Carnaval* took precedence.

During the four nights of *Carnaval*, women wore masks called *capuchas* (hoods) that completely covered their heads and shoulders, a disguise that gave them anonymity. With a license to misbehave during this time of wild abandon, the *mascaritas* (masked women) took full advantage of the freedom to let loose, but sometimes it was to their detriment. Statistics for rape spiked during *Carnaval*, and I was warned of the danger.

My landlady's friend made a mask for me of shiny blue taffeta that fit loosely over my head with seductively-shaped eye holes, a down-turned, slightly open red mouth, and frowning black eyebrows that suggested a no-nonsense attitude. Tight-fitting white slacks and a sleeveless orange-patterned blouse completed my *mascarita* outfit.

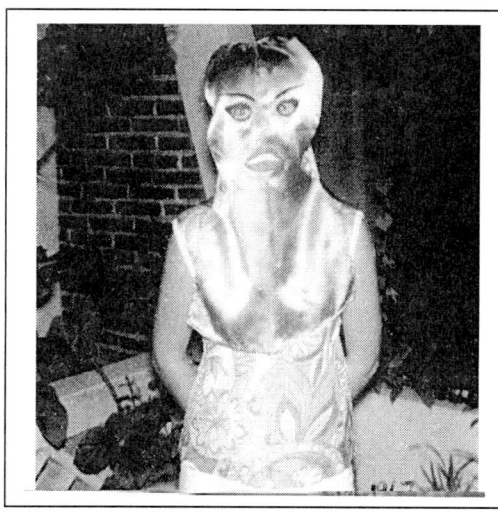

When I tried on my *Carnaval* mask in the inner courtyard of my house, I thought it was beautiful.
February 1967

All the action during *Carnaval* took place at *El Caballito,* so I hailed a taxi and joined the parade of jeeps heading to the club. The air inside the mask was stuffy, and the eye holes blocked some of my vision, but that would be the least of my problems. When I entered the club, I realized my mask was all wrong. It looked nothing like the other masks, and the large cut-out eye holes betrayed my blue eyes and blonde hair, giving away my identity. The other women wore *capuchas* made of patterned cotton fabric that fit tightly like a glove over their heads with narrow eye slits and no mouth or eyebrows. That's what I needed.

The next night, my Bolivian friend Nelva gave me a beige cotton *capucha* with little blue flowers, and this time no one recognized me. All the *mascaritas* spoke in a high-pitch to disguise their real voices which was a boon for me, because it hid my accent. If I said very little and didn't make any grammatical errors, the men thought I was a local girl.

As a result, they treated me in a more familiar, informal way than the polite, distant manner I usually experienced. Being accepted as a local girl broke down barriers and gave me a peek into another aspect of the culture. It reminded me of the princess played by Audrey Hepburn in the movie *Roman Holiday* who fled the palace to experience Rome as an ordinary person and loved the freedom it brought.

El Caballito was packed wall to wall with people and decorated with brightly-colored lights, flowers, streamers, confetti, and green palm fronds. The festive, non-stop music alternated between lively Santa Cruz *taquirari* dance music played on trumpets, saxophones, clarinets, drums, and tubas and Brazilian *Carnaval* music of warm, vibrant *samba* rhythms played on trumpets, saxophones, drums, gongs, bells, rattles, tambourines, and whistles.

I danced with my friend John and as he looked me up and down, I laughed to myself because he obviously didn't recognize me. When I teased Archie, he appeared puzzled, trying to figure out who I was, until I whispered in his ear, *"Soy Peggy"* (I'm Peggy), which gave him a frightful shock and a surprised laugh.

Women had the upper hand, and I felt in control for a change. As a *mascarita,* I rode that wave of confidence and relished the feeling of empowerment, but the wave eventually crashed in an unexpected and frightening way.

Until then, however, I danced with several partners. One night I chose a cute, dark-haired young man from France named Guy (pronounced Gēē) who taught French at the Alliance Francaise. Toward the end of the evening, we left the club and went back to his house where I removed my mask. We continued speaking Spanish, now in hushed tones, and I got home late.

On the final night of the festival, I again wore the *capucha* and set my sights on a slim, handsome, young Bolivian man with light brown eyes and light brown hair. His name was Lucho, and we danced and laughed. I was very attracted to him, and at one point, he grabbed my hand and led me outside to his four-wheel-drive pickup truck which he drove into the *campo.* I was all caught up with the excitement of *Carnaval* and wondered where we were going.

But that changed when he stopped the truck in the middle of nowhere, turned off the lights, and started pulling at my clothes. "No, no," I said, pushing his hands away. What was I doing with this guy, anyway? I hardly knew him. I was stupid to leave the club. What was I thinking? Was I going to be one of those statistics I had heard about?

As I pushed him away, Lucho asked, "*Eres* birhain*?*" "*Cómo?*" (Pardon?), I responded. I knew "*Eres*" meant "Are you," but I didn't understand the last word. He urgently repeated, "*Eres* birhain*?* *Eres* birhain*?*" If there was ever a time to understand Spanish, this was it. I was scared. He asked again and again. And finally it came to me -- he was asking, "*Eres virgen?*" (Are you a virgin?) "*Sí,sí*" (Yes, yes), I squeaked in my high-pitched *mascarita* voice, still staying in character. But I didn't want to be a *mascarita* any more. I just wanted to be me.

The charade was over anyway. Lucho had figured out who I really was and without saying another word, turned on the ignition and took me home, where I bid him a good night, breathed a sigh of relief, and hung up my *Carnaval* mask for good.

CHAPTER TWENTY-SIX
LUCHO

At the end of February 1967, after our saga of mixed signals during *Carnaval,* Lucho and I spoke again in the plaza. The first time he had ever seen me, he confided, was in La Paz at the University of San Andrés. He boasted that he was the one who had rescued me from my classroom when the door was stuck and had followed me to the front lobby, where I met a young American man "*con pelo rojo*" (with red hair). Ah, yes, my red-headed boyfriend Kevin had met me there that evening. I was struck by this amazing coincidence and looked at Lucho with renewed interest.

He was, after all, very handsome and funny, sometimes a bit loud, but with a mischievous sense of humor, charm, intelligence, energy, and a confident stride that was sexy and attractive.

His full name was actually Luis Roberto Velasco Suarez, but everyone called him Lucho. I didn't know it at the time, but his family was part of the old *Cruceño* aristocracy, and his ancestors from southern Spain were among the original settlers of Santa Cruz. One of his ancestors, José Miguel de Velasco, was born in Santa Cruz in 1795 and served as President of Bolivia four times between 1828 and 1848.

When Lucho invited me to go on a trip to the *campo*, I decided to give him another chance. It was a sunny afternoon when Lucho came by in his four-wheel-drive pickup truck accompanied by another couple, but he was an hour late. It took another half hour to travel five miles (at 10 mph) on dusty, unpaved, uneven, rutted roads into the *campo* past open fields scattered with trees and through small towns of narrow streets and one-story, white-washed Spanish colonial houses with extended red-tile roofs supported by simple wooden columns.

Finally, we arrived at a sandy river bed bordered on one side by a creek. This was the River Piraí (which means "river of fish" in the Guaraní Indian language), but at this time of year, the water was low. During the wet season, the river flooded the sandy area. This was the closest river to the city of Santa Cruz and was a popular place to cool off and swim. But as we walked around, Lucho accidentally knocked my purse into a puddle of water. He apologized and quickly spread everything out to dry, and as we posed for the photo on the opposite page, my purse and its contents were lying on the ground behind us.

I was relieved when our trip back to Santa Cruz was uneventful and Lucho's pickup truck didn't get stuck in the mud, a typical occurrence when traveling on rural *campo* roads. When that happened, everyone but the driver got out and pushed. Living in the high altitude of the Andes was the greatest adjustment to life in La Paz, but here in Santa Cruz, traveling on unpaved roads was the biggest challenge, and it helped to have a sense of humor.

One afternoon, I settled into my seat at the *Cine Palace* (Movie Palace) to watch the "spaghetti western" *For a Few Dollars More* starring Clint Eastwood. The movie was in English with Spanish subtitles, and the theater was packed. In one of the early scenes in a small town in the American West of the 1890s, I was startled at how much the dusty unpaved streets, hitching posts, and raised sidewalks looked like Santa Cruz. As I stifled a laugh, a man in the theater shouted out, "Santa Cruz! Santa Cruz!," and the audience erupted in laughter. But the wild-West frontier image of the city was about to change.

An ambitious construction project to pave the streets began around the central plaza as hexagon-shaped, interlocking pavers were installed, creating a honeycomb pattern. The 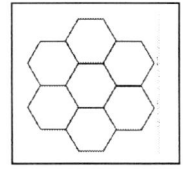 street around the plaza was completed by the time I left Santa Cruz, and the project continued onto adjacent streets.

As each side of the plaza was finished, I couldn't wait to step off the sidewalk, stamp my feet on the new surface, and cross the pavement to the other side. The streets were a novelty and felt so luxurious. They were the most beautiful streets I had ever seen, and the local *Cruceños* were proud of their modern look.

In the above photo, Lucho (left) and a friend cross the southwest corner of the plaza. The Basilica de San Lorenzo towers overhead, and the archway of *La Pascana* is in the distance where piles of dirt indicate continued street construction. Below is another view of the newly-paved street around the central plaza.

CHAPTER TWENTY-SEVEN
MEETING THE CHIEF JUSTICE

Although Santa Cruz was not as modern as La Paz or Cochabamba, it was chosen for a visit by Chief Justice Earl Warren of the U.S. Supreme Court who was on a tour of South America.

But before arriving in Santa Cruz, Warren traveled to Sucre, Bolivia on March 14, 1967 to speak at a session of the Bolivian Supreme Court. Bolivian President René Barrientos accompanied him, and

Chief Justice
Earl Warren

the town turned out to welcome the highest U.S. official to ever visit.

Chief Justice Warren spoke about the U.S. Constitution as a document that has preserved democracy in the U.S. and how peace through law must be established in order to build justice. His speech was warmly received, and he praised Barrientos as a man who respected law and freedom.

After his visit to Sucre, Earl Warren asked to meet with Peace Corps Volunteers, so the next day, he and President Barrientos flew to Santa Cruz. Our city was chosen because of its low elevation and out of concern for the Chief Justice's heart condition. Very quickly, 20 Volunteers were rounded up to meet with Earl Warren in a large room at a USAID guest house where he was staying.

Earl Warren, with his white hair, warm, friendly eyes, and easy smile, wore an open-collared shirt as he sat down to talk with us. His calm, down-to-earth manner put us all at ease. He said how proud he was of us and went around the room, asking each one to describe the work he or she was doing. He listened intently and asked questions, interested in every detail. For example, one Volunteer was working in a tuberculosis eradication program, another was teaching English, and a third was helping to build a small school, and so on. But when Earl Warren came to me, and I described my job as a Volunteer secretary in the Peace Corps office, he was momentarily confused but nodded his head and went on to the next person.

Then he spoke about the responsibility of government to its people and how important it was to take care of everyone. Earl Warren was kind, thoughtful and articulate, an optimist who saw the good in people and felt empathy toward those who were suffering. We were all tremendously impressed with him and his vision, and as we said goodbye, we felt lucky to have met this exceptional man.

CHAPTER TWENTY-EIGHT
SEARCHING FOR CHE GUEVARA

Rumors continued that Che Guevara and his band of guerrillas were prowling the rural lowlands and mountains of the Department of Santa Cruz, but Bolivian President René Barrientos denied it. However, at the end of March 1967, after a skirmish between

Che Guevara

the Bolivian army and the guerrillas, Barrientos acknowledged their existence, and American military advisers and armaments arrived in Santa Cruz to assist the Bolivian army.

Journalists from around the world also arrived in Santa Cruz. One afternoon in early April 1967, Big Al and a younger man named George burst into the office laughing after Big Al had picked him up at the airport. They were good friends and knew each other from Peace Corps training camp in Puerto Rico where George had taught Spanish to the trainees. Big Al introduced George to Archie and me, and they retired to Big Al's office and closed the door.

George, a good-looking, dark-haired young man of average height, was a freelance Anglo-Chilean journalist. Sensing a big story in Santa Cruz and hoping to interview Che, he flew there from Santiago, Chile.

᠊n my desk across the hall, I watched as George and Big Al emerged from their meeting and stopped at Archie's desk. Archie bent down to spin the combination dial of the safe and placed George's passport and American money inside. Then Archie spread out a map and described the terrain in the Department of Santa Cruz. The semi-desert to the south, he told George, was not a likely place to find Che because there was no place to hide, but the jungle to the north was a better bet. In high spirits, George said goodbye, and we wished him well as he headed into the *campo* in search of Che's guerrilla camp. But the next time I saw George, nearly three months later, I would barely recognize him.

The military action against the guerrillas took place 50-150 miles southwest of the city of Santa Cruz, so our daily life went on as usual. Lucho and I continued dating, going to movies and parties, dancing at *El Caballito,* and relaxing at *La Pascana.* Also relaxing at *La Pascana* were American military forces, but the behavior of some embarrassed us, because they were rude and loud. Instead of ordering *cerveza* (beer) from a waiter, they would shout out in English to anyone, "Get me another beer." Nevertheless, they provided valuable assistance and trained the Bolivian Army Rangers who were crushing the guerrilla movement.

Eight days after George went into the *campo* in search of Che, Archie and Marty were married on April 14, 1967 at *La Iglesia de la Santa Cruz* (The Church of the Holy Cross). All the Volunteers in the area and Archie's large family attended. Big Al walked Marty down the aisle, and she looked beautiful in her white, French lace wedding dress made by one of Lucho's cousins. The dress I wore to the wedding was also made by a local seamstress from a picture I clipped out of a magazine. There were no dress shops in Santa Cruz, so this was the common practice. Two months later, the newlyweds flew to Cincinnati, Ohio for another reception and to introduce Archie to Marty's family.

I posed with Marty and Archie at their wedding reception in a hall at the church in Santa Cruz, April 14, 1967.

Marty reminded me of myself because she, too, was looking for adventure when she accepted a position to teach second grade in Bolivia in 1965. The job was at the American School run by the U.S. Government and Gulf Oil for the Bolivian and American children of its workers in a region rich in petroleum and natural gas.

Marty first met Archie when the Bolivian family she lived with invited Archie, their next-door neighbor, to meet the tall, pretty, blonde American. When one of daughters asked Archie what he thought of Marty, he assumed Marty didn't understand Spanish and noticing her large feet, he wondered aloud what her shoe size was. Marty answered, "*Ocho y medio*" (eight and a half), embarrassing Archie so much that he made an extra effort to befriend Marty, and their friendship grew into romance.

Six days after their wedding, on April 20, 1967, we were alarmed to hear that our journalist friend George and two other men suspected of collaborating with the guerrillas were arrested by military authorities as they walked through the town of Muyupampa (149 miles south of Santa Cruz). Communication in the *campo* was poor, and first reports indicated they had been killed, but their photo in the *Presencia* newspaper the following day confirmed they were alive.

Before being arrested, George had been frustrated at traveling with military patrols through abandoned guerrilla camps, so one night he slipped through the military guard into guerrilla territory where he met two children who guided him to Che's camp. However, the guerrillas distrusted George and never allowed him to meet Che.

The day after arriving in camp, George was ordered to leave with two men who had met several times with Che and sympathized with his cause. They were Régis Debray, a French intellectual, and Ciro Roberto Bustos, an Argentine artist. Using George as cover, the two men posed as journalists. But all three were arrested and physically beaten in Muyupampa, with Debray and Bustos receiving the most brutal treatment. In an article years later, George remembered the floor of his cell became a sewer and the food was so horrible he went on a hunger strike for four days. Meanwhile, the national and foreign press asked what had happened to the three men, but little was released, and we worried about our friend.

A couple of months passed during which we heard reports of continued skirmishes between the Bolivian army and the guerrillas, but nothing of George until one sunny morning, a frail, bearded young man appeared in the Peace Corps office followed by a tall Bolivian army officer. As they stood in the hallway between my office and Archie's, I gasped! It was George, emaciated and hollow-eyed with sunken-in cheeks. I jumped up from my desk, ran over to him, and asked, "George, all you all right? We've been so worried about you?" In a dazed, flat voice, George murmured, "Is Big Al here?" "No, he's in the *campo*," I answered. "And Archie?" he wondered. "No, he's in the states on his honeymoon. I'm the only one here," I replied. Frowning with disappointment, George slowly nodded his head, then looked at me and asked, "Can I talk to you?"

"Yes, please, have a seat," I said, motioning to a chair in my office as I sat down at my desk. The stern Bolivian army officer followed and stood behind George, looking down at us with his hands clasped behind his back. I continued asking George how he was and telling him of our concern for him when he suddenly cut me short and said in a very even tone, "This man is watching us very carefully. Don't act so concerned about me. Just talk in an everyday, conversational voice."

Obviously, the officer didn't understand English, so I put on a bright face and spoke in a lighter tone about ather, Archie's wedding, and the paving of the main street around the central plaza. I even smiled up at the Bolivian army officer, but he didn't smile back. Was George still under arrest? Was the officer there to verify George had contacts in the Peace Corps office? I didn't know and couldn't ask. After ten minutes, George and the army official said goodbye and left the office.

Shortly thereafter, to my relief, I heard George was set free on July 8, 1967 and flew to La Paz. However, the other two men, Debray and Bustos, were given 30-year sentences after a trial in August, but due to an international campaign, they were released three years later.

Because of George's early release, rumors circulated that he was actually a CIA agent, but whether he was or not, he certainly paid dearly for venturing out on his own in search of the elusive Che Guevara.

CHAPTER TWENTY-NINE
MORE CULTURE SHOCK

La Choquita was Lucho's nickname for me, which he translated as "the baby blonde." I was smitten. In my favorite photo of us taken in April 1967 at the home of one of his friends, I held Lucho close and snuggled against his neck. We were in love.

Most of our evenings were spent together after I finished work. Lucho didn't have a regular job, but he often went out of town. What he did on those trips was a mystery to me. When I asked him about it, his answer was simply "*negocios*" (business) and nothing more.

During one of those trips, I entered a dance contest at *La Pascana* with a Bolivian male friend. We danced to live band music, and the audience voted by applause, choosing us as the winners. I was offered the choice of two prizes -- *una serenata* (a serenade) or *una botella de champaña* (a bottle of champagne). I loved the romantic, Latin custom of a serenade, so

.√nat I chose. But as the runners-up cheered
..ıd popped open the bubbly wine to celebrate, I
realized my mistake, especially because the serenade
never materialized.

I complained about this slight to Lucho when he
returned, and the next night, male voices singing
Spanish songs on the street outside my house woke
me up as I was dozing off. The music drifted through
the courtyard into my bedroom window, and I
wondered if it was for me. The loudest singer
sounded like Lucho, but was it? Without a balcony to
see who was singing, I wasn't sure. Should I open
the front door in my pajamas? What if the serenade
wasn't for me? But it was, and when Lucho took
credit for it the next day, I loved him even more.

Las Palmas (The Palms), a private country club in
Santa Cruz, was built in the early 1960s by Gulf Oil
for its employees and their families. Local families
also joined, and Lucho's was one of them. In May
1967, he invited me to the club for an afternoon swim
in the beautiful blue, chlorinated swimming pool and a
dance that evening. The only other pool of its kind in
Bolivia was at the USAID guest house where Chief
Justice Earl Warren had stayed. But while swimming,
I watched as the pearl ring I bought in Rio de Janeiro
floated off my finger and sank to the bottom of the
pool. Lucho tried to find it several times, but the ring
was gone.

That evening, Lucho and I arrived at the club for the
dance held on the terrace outside, but as we
approached the gathering, Lucho suddenly stopped,
grabbed my arm, and pulled me into the shadows.
He saw at the head table Bolivian President René

Barrientos, a gallant-looking, dark-haired man in his late 40s casually dressed in a short-sleeved white shirt and dark slacks. Lucho whispered that Barrientos was going to pick the prettiest girl to sit with him and predicted it would be me so Barrientos could practice his English. I said I wouldn't mind, but Lucho was having none of it, so we snuck in the back entrance and sat

René Barrientos

all alone at the far end of the terrace surrounded by empty tables covered with white tablecloths.

Soon enough, President Barrientos was giving all his attention to a very beautiful, dark-haired young woman seated next to him. She had recently won the Miss Santa Cruz beauty contest. Now it was safe to leave our table and dance, which is when this photo was taken, and Barrientos never saw me.

Lucho lived around the corner from my house with his parents, a younger brother named Raúl, his grandmother, and his dog, a female boxer named *Brisa* (breeze). Traditionally in Latin cultures, children lived with their parents until they married. At Lucho's home, a wrought-iron gate at the entrance opened onto a concrete ramp (where a vehicle was parked) and led up to the front double-doors and into a large,

ved, inner courtyard of potted plants and
uden benches around which all the rooms were
located.

It was here one afternoon that I met Lucho's
grandmother, a tiny, elderly, gray-haired woman
wearing a black dress. As she sat hunched over a
table and reminisced about her deceased husband,
she talked about his many exploits as a seducer of
women during their marriage. My sympathy for her
turned into confusion, however, when I realized she
was actually boasting about his machismo. I was
shocked she was proud of his many conquests.

A few days later, Archie told me he saw Lucho's
younger sister in the plaza. When I said Lucho didn't
have a younger sister, Archie explained she was from
the second family Lucho's father had in town.
Infidelity was openly accepted in Latin cultures, and
since Lucho and I had talked about marrying some
day, I wondered if he would behave as his father and
grandfather had.

When I posed that question to him, he said, of course
he would, but I would always be "*número uno*"
(number one). I was shocked he could be so open
about being unfaithful, but men in Latin cultures were
raised to have extramarital affairs as a way to prove
their masculinity and demonstrate their sexual
appetite, whereas women were raised to accept
infidelity as a way to keep the family together,
because family came first. But that was a role I could
never play, and when I told Lucho how I felt, it was his
turn to be shocked. The clash of cultures was a
sobering revelation for both of us.

CHAPTER THIRTY
VAYA CON DIOS (GO WITH GOD)

My Peace Corps service was coming to an end on August 6, 1967, a national holiday celebrating Bolivia's independence from Spain in 1825, but before leaving Santa Cruz, I trained my replacement, a Peace Corps Volunteer secretary from Puerto Rico named Ruth, a pleasant young woman with long dark hair. And when I made my airline reservation to go to La Paz for final checkout, Lucho decided to go with me. After two years, I was excited to be going home.

Meanwhile, southwest of Santa Cruz, Che Guevara had failed to inspire the *campesinos* who instead reported his whereabouts to the Bolivian army. The *campesinos* distrusted foreigners such as Che and admired President René Barrientos, a man of mixed Quechua and Spanish descent, so revolution was unlikely.

With the revolution failing, the guerrillas were desperate for food and medicine and stopped a bus on the road between Santa Cruz and Cochabamba in July 1967. Among the passengers were a Peace Corps married couple assigned to the Santa Cruz *campo*. After the guerrillas received their supplies, all the passengers were released, but the incident gave the Peace Corps a momentary scare.

Back home in Santa Cruz on my final afternoon, I was packing my luggage when I gave in to temptation. My landlady, *Señora* Virginia, offered me some vanilla ice cream, as she had many times before, and this time I accepted. After denying myself for too long, I slowly savored the rich creamy taste of the frozen treat and breathed a sigh of relief when there were no ill effects.

The next day, in the early morning darkness of August 1, 1967, the *Señora* and I were waiting outside for Lucho to come by in a taxi to go to the airport, but he was late. When I called his house, I urged him to hurry, *"Es la hora. Vámonos!"* (It's time. Let's go!), and Lucho was on his way. After he loaded my luggage into the taxi, I hugged the *Señora* goodbye, and when she whispered in my ear, *"Vaya con Dios,"* (Go with God), I had tears in my eyes.

At the airport, the early rays of sunshine reflected off the LAB Airline DC-3 as Lucho and I walked across the tarmac to board, and I saw the old man with a clubfoot waiting by his shoeshine stand for customers. When the plane rose in the sky, I took one last look down at the lush green landscape and said goodbye to charming Santa Cruz, a city unspoiled by modern civilization.

After our plane landed at the El Alto Airport, the noise and fast pace of the vibrant city of La Paz greeted us as we rode in a taxi down the mountain to Lucho's small, modestly furnished, one bedroom, one bath apartment where I stayed for several days. In the living room, a 45 rpm record player on the bookcase caught my eye. Among the small collection of 45 rpm records, I found one I especially liked by Lucho Gatica, a Chilean ballad singer, and I played it so often that Lucho gave me the record to take home.

Final paperwork at the Peace Corps office was completed, and a medical checkup showed amoebas and worms in my intestinal system, a common malady. Treatment required strong medication in the form of a big red pill and fasting for most of the day, which left me nauseous and irritable, but it worked.

One final task remained, picking up my plane ticket at the Braniff Airlines office next to the Hotel La Paz. On the sidewalk in front of the office, I bumped into George, the reporter who had been jailed under suspicion of collaborating with Che Guevara. He looked handsome, rested, and relaxed, having shaved his beard and gained some weight, and after chatting a few minutes, he asked me to go out with him that evening. I was tempted but confessed I was in La Paz with my Bolivian boyfriend and couldn't. I still wonder what hair-raising tales he would have shared about his search for Che and subsequent incarceration.

That evening, Lucho and I dined at the two-story home of his older sister, Sonia, a tall, pretty woman in her late 20s with light brown hair. She was an airline stewardess on LAB Airlines, and her husband was a pilot with the Bolivian Air Force, but he was absent that evening. Sonia served us a lovely dinner and warmly welcomed me as part of the family.

Pablo, a friend of Lucho's who often hung out with us in Santa Cruz, was also in La Paz. A well-educated young man with dark wavy hair, he dressed elegantly and spoke English fluently. One sunny afternoon, the three of us sat at a table under a large umbrella at a sidewalk café in front of the Copacabana Hotel. As the men drank beer and I sipped 7Up, we watched the passing parade of pedestrians and traffic along the Prado in the highest capital city in the world. I had sat there many times before, but this would be the last time, and Lucho and I were feeling the pinch as our days together were coming to an end.

| (L-R) Me, Pablo, and Lucho at the sidewalk café in front of the Copacabana Hotel on the Prado in La Paz, 1967. | (L-R) Pablo, me, and Lucho at the *Galey* nightclub in La Paz, 1967. |

My final evening in Bolivia was spent with Lucho and Pablo at the *Galey* nightclub listening to the beautiful, haunting melodies of Andean folklore music. Four male musicians wearing woven wool ponchos of vibrant red and yellow stripes and colorful, woven wool hats with ear flaps played highland musical instruments -- wooden panpipes, flutes, drums, guitars, and the *charango* (a ten-stringed instrument resembling a small guitar traditionally made from the shell of an armadillo). The soulful music of the ancient Aymara culture made for a nostalgic evening.

My last morning, Bolivia's Independence Day, was a bright Sunday, and Lucho bought me a copy of the extra-thick newspaper so I could read all about the Bolivian holiday on the plane. Pablo joined us, and we rode to the La Paz airport arriving in good time, but as I was checking in at the airline counter, Lucho said he would join me at the boarding gate and left.

While waiting at the gate with Pablo, I saw a beautiful lemon-yellow Braniff jet plane sitting on the tarmac as passengers climbed up the stairway ramp to board. But time was ticking away and I wondered where Lucho was. It was getting later and later, and Pablo left to find him, but now it was only minutes before I had to board. Suddenly, Pablo ran back, yelling for me to get on the plane. "But I haven't said goodbye to Lucho," I cried. "Where is he?" Looking disgusted, Pablo said Lucho wasn't going to say goodbye to me. "Why?" I asked. Pablo shook his head and said, "Because you're leaving him." I sighed, but it was time to go, so I hugged Pablo goodbye and trudged out to the plane, taking one last look around for Lucho, but to no avail. What a way to end my two years in Bolivia.

As the jet plane coasted endlessly on the extra-long runway and finally rose in the thin air, I looked down at the majestic mountains, rugged *altiplano* landscape, and the bowl-shaped capital city of La Paz which held so many precious memories for me. And in spite of Lucho's antics, I was happy to be going home to America.

POSTSCRIPT
I soon received a letter of apology from Lucho, and we corresponded for a year, but he didn't want to

come to the states, and I wasn't ready to return to Bolivia. Our letters became fewer and fewer, and eventually we went our separate ways, but I still think of him with much affection.

Two months after I left Bolivia, on October 8, 1967, Che Guevara was captured by the Bolivian Rangers near the small village of La Higuera (50 miles southwest of Santa Cruz), imprisoned in a schoolhouse, and under orders from President Barrientos, shot and killed the next day.

Two years later in 1969, President René Barrientos died in a helicopter crash near Cochabamba.

In 1971, Bolivia threw the Peace Corps out of the country, allowing it to return in 1990. But in 2008, the Peace Corps left the country on its own due to political instability.

And by the year 2000, Santa Cruz had become Bolivia's largest and richest city, beautifully lined with paved streets and a skyline of tall buildings.

Forty-five years after leaving Bolivia, I still treasure the two years I lived there as the most challenging and exciting of my life, and I thank Bolivia, its people, and the Peace Corps for a priceless experience.

THE END